DATE			

voices

of the

EARTH

Lifetouch

About the Author

Clea Danaan's articles on gardening and environmental activism have appeared in *Sage Woman* and *Organic Family*. Danaan's previous book, *Sacred Land*, was a finalist for the 2007 *ForeWord* Book of the Year (Mind/Body/Spirit category) and won a bronze medal 2008 Independent Publisher Book Award for "Most Likely to Save the Planet." She lives in Colorado.

voices

of the

EARTH

THE

PATH OF

GREEN SPIRITUALITY

CLEA DANAAN

Llewellyn Publications
Woodbury, Minnesota

First Edition
First Printing, 2009

Cover design by Ellen Dahl
Cover background image © Digital Stock
Editing by Nicole Edman
Interior book design by Joanna Willis
Interior illustrations by Llewellyn art department

Llewellyn is a registered trademark of Llewellyn Worldwide, Ltd.

LIBRARY OF CONGRESS CATALOGING-IN-PUBLICATION DATA
Danaan, Clea.
  Voices of the earth: the path of green spirituality / Clea Danaan. — 1st ed.
     p. cm.
  Includes bibliographical references.
  ISBN 978-0-7387-1465-3
  1. Nature—Religious aspects. 2. Nature—Psychic aspects. I. Title.
  BL65.N35D36 2009
  202'.12—dc22
                                                        2008040891

Llewellyn Worldwide does not participate in, endorse, or have any authority or responsibility concerning private business transactions between our authors and the public.
   All mail addressed to the author is forwarded but the publisher cannot, unless specifically instructed by the author, give out an address or phone number.
   Any Internet references contained in this work are current at publication time, but the publisher cannot guarantee that a specific location will continue to be maintained. Please refer to the publisher's website for links to authors' websites and other sources.

Llewellyn Publications
A Division of Llewellyn Worldwide, Ltd.
2143 Wooddale Drive, Dept. 978-0-7387-1465-3
Woodbury, MN 55125-2989, U.S.A.
www.llewellyn.com

Printed in the United States of America

ALSO BY CLEA DANAAN

Sacred Land:
Intuitive Gardening for Personal,
Political & Environmental Change

CONTENTS

INTRODUCTION

*W*hen my daughter was only a few days old, I took her outside and put her, naked, in the shade of an elder. Her tiny body melted into the ground, feeling the support that only the earth can give.

"This is the earth," I told her. "Great Earth, I pledge my daughter to you. I give you thanks for the gift of her life."

She kicked, content, gazing at me with her steel-blue newborn eyes. The dappled autumn sunlight scattered leaf patterns on her perfect skin. I lay down beside her and nursed her, our cheeks pressing into the grass.

At birth, she screamed with scrunchy pink anger at the abrupt shift in environments. She slept lightly and cried often. She was what some people call a colicky baby; I believe she had not yet felt ready to inhabit her little body. But there on the grass that day, nursing, gazing at the trees, cuddling into the solid ground beneath her, the indignation and frustration melted away. She felt, for the afternoon, at peace.

As humans, our first relationship is with our mother— the mother who birthed us, and also the Mother Earth.

Before birth, we know the pull of gravity. We learn to dance with two bodies: the mother womb around us and the planet beneath. Once we slip from the salty waters of our conception, we become air-breathing terrestrials. The umbilical cord is cut, but we will remain attached to the placenta of the earth until we die.

Babies seem to know this connection instinctively. Take a crying baby outside, and as long as she is fed, dry, and not in pain, she will often calm instantly. Outside she can breathe. She can feel the breeze on her skin, hear the birds, and touch the soil with her tiny body. She instinctively loves the natural world.

Our bodies and souls love the natural world, and only very recently have our minds disconnected from the natural currents of life on our planet. In our highly technological, capitalistic culture, we have largely lost touch with changing season, the sources of our food, and the living land. This disconnect is an illness. While there is nothing inherently wrong with money and technology, when we divorce our conscious awareness from our roots, we become zombies. Instead of being controlled by an evil sorcerer, we are driven by our inner demons of greed, fear, and narcissism.

Many people and organizations have developed an awareness of this illness. We are realizing we cannot continue to rape and plunder the earth as we have been doing. Green living and environmental organizations are now becoming mainstream. If you have enough money, you can "green" anything: your house, car, food, clothes, even investments.

Greater environmental awareness is crucial, but these market-based solutions are incomplete: there is a deeper aspect to living in harmony on earth. In order to live in right relationship with the natural world—and with our own selves, which are of course a part of nature—we must learn to connect with nature spiritually. By this I mean more than just meditating outdoors or taking more camping trips or growing your own vegetables. These are important behaviors, but we can go deeper.

I am a nature intuitive. Through my work as a healer, artist, and nature lover, I have developed the ability to talk to plants, the wind, stones, and rivers. I am teaching my daughter not only how to feel good being outside, but how to have a real relationship with nature. I can teach you to do the same. When you develop the ability to talk to nature, you will be living a truly green life. You will go beyond environmental stewardship and become an Earth Ally, one who will lead the planet to wholeness.

Developing deep awareness of the earth and our own souls constitutes a power-filled spiritual path. This book is a guide to developing your own spiritually based path as a nature mystic by forming a psychic connection to the land. I will walk you through all aspects of the life of a nature intuitive, from gardening to working with herbs and plant spirits to a more holistic awareness of your clothing, home, and food. Through this work, you will awaken your psychic powers and be able to talk to nature—and you'll be able to hear her reply. Your ability to talk to Nature will have far-reaching consequences as you learn to love more deeply. When you open yourself to the wisdom of nature, you will find healing and renewal in the midst of a crazy world. Through deep listening, you will find your own soul. You will also discover tools to face the overwhelming reality of living in a sensitive body in the midst of wars, corporate greed, fear, loneliness, and all the challenges of humankind.

Anyone can learn to sense subtle energies in trees, stones, rivers, and the wind. *Voices of the Earth* is a guide to this awakening consciousness. John Welwood writes, "Awareness born of love is the only force that can bring healing and renewal."[1] With this awareness will come a more fulfilling life based on truly, deeply "green" principles that transcend fads and require no monetary contribution. This awareness goes beyond following certain behaviors, such as recycling, to living a transformed life of wholeness and deep vision.

Do you feel disconnected from other people? From your life path? Do you have trouble loving yourself? Do you suffer from anxiety, depression, and daily worry? Learning to expand your awareness to the spiritual aspects of nature and the universe will help you find wholeness and healing. You will be able to find your path, your life's work. You will know a deep love from the universe and the planet, and you'll be able to take that love in, then

---

1. Welwood, *Love and Awakening*, 20.

share it with others. You will have tools to live more powerfully in a time of fear and chaos. All of these gifts can come from having a deep, intuitive, psychic relationship with Nature and Spirit.

Each chapter of this book offers exercises and meditations to help you deepen your spiritual practice with nature; meditations are marked with a dingbat (❧). Those with experience in ritual and meditation will find the basic outline of the exercises familiar—most are guided meditations designed to help you open psychically to the land and other forces. The guided meditations always begin with grounding and centering, which means connecting your energy to the earth and to your core. A simple way to ground is to picture roots of energy growing from your base chakra (or the sacral area at the base of your spine) down into the ground. When you feel a heaviness in your hips, like a magnet pulling you toward the ground, you are "grounded." After grounding, you will also feel an increased clarity and focus. To center, take a few breaths, paying attention to the air as it enters your lungs, pauses, exhales, and again pauses. Centering brings your attention into your body and the present moment. It can be used to calm yourself, focus your attention if you feel scattered, or prepare for meditation and ritual. Use your breath as you read this book to center, ground, and connect with your spirit.

Meditation brings us into altered states, or trances. A trance is just altered consciousness. We enter trance states frequently, often without realizing. If you have ever been driving and realize you have no recollection of the past ten miles, or if you have gotten lost in a daydream, or entered a deep calm while gardening, making love, or cooking, then you know simple trance states. Deeper trance work, achieved by shamans or through mind-altering substances, is not necessary for the kind of work in this book and should only be done by experienced practitioners. The light trance states you enter through the meditations offered here should, however, be approached mindfully. Remember always to return to everyday space after meditation.

One gradual way to return to normal waking consciousness is through art, including painting, dance, or writing. While art can bring you into an altered state, it can also be a bridge between spirit work and everyday interactions. I will remind you after each meditation to put your thoughts in writing in a journal where you can record your processes, thoughts, dreams, and discoveries. By writing or drawing in your journal, include reflections on the practices and any thoughts or feelings that emerge. I have included a list of journal exercises at the end of the book for you to revisit. Let your journal be a place to free-write about your psychic journey as well. Return to your journal regularly, as it will help you process your work and keep a record of your progress.

At the end of each chapter I will offer you an exercise, art project, and journal topic related to that chapter's story and discussion. Explore these in your own time, as you feel drawn to them. They are intended for individual work, but you might also want to work through them with a friend or a group. Some of the activities may feel more advanced than where you currently are on the path of green spirituality; do whatever parts of them you feel able to do, without self-judgment. Other activities may feel too basic; that is fine—take what is of value to you, and perhaps revisit the rest at a later time.

The Art as Meditation project offered at the end of the chapter will access your right brain, the part of us open to images and unconscious information. The point is not to make perfect art (whatever that is), but to express your heart through a creative project. I offer fairly simple instructions; feel free to make your crafts as elaborate as you like. Use lots of symbols, colors, and materials that make you happy, that feel sensuous and fun. Let the project be a celebration of your connection with Spirit and the land. Matthew Fox says, "Art is not for art's sake, but for ecstasy's sake."[2] Make your art an offering to the Creator from the creator in you.

I tell my daughter often as she learns to drink from a big-girl cup to go slow, go slow. When I studied craniosacral therapy (an alternative therapy using light touch to restore misaligned bones and ease nerve restriction), my teacher instructed that if we could not feel the very subtle body rhythm, we needed to lighten our touch. An art teacher in college encouraged us to look, then look again. As you read, as you explore your own intuition and energetic sensitivity,

2. Fox, *A Spirituality Named Compassion*, 109.

hold all of these lessons in mind: slow way down, lighten your touch, and look again. Rushing and forcing will not help you grow as a psychic or a spiritual initiate. Trust. Open. Breathe.

I wish for you through this work the joy of lying in the grass on a sunny day balanced with the excitement of advanced spiritual evolution. May it take you far in your soul, heart, and life. Let us begin!

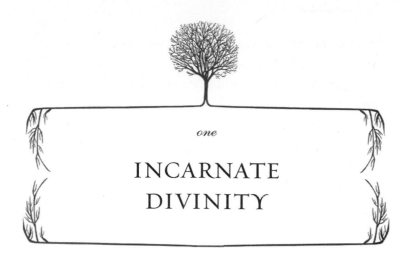

one

INCARNATE
DIVINITY

I needed some fresh air and solitude. I was at a retreat center in Redmond, Washington, studying Expressive Arts Therapy. It had been an intense weekend of personal discovery, and I decided to use what was left of the lunch break to decompress. The nearby wetland beckoned. Winter cattails poked through the mud, brown alder leaves pasted the soggy ground, and though it was afternoon, hoar frost still lurked at the clearing edges. Blackberry bushes in winter have their own unique smell, sweet and grassy, often laced with the clay scent of popping wetland soil. My body expanded into the land around me, and my muscles relaxed. I felt free and light as my footsteps landed on the springy ground, my mind open and soft.

I followed the edge of the creek as it meandered through faded marsh grass and winter-bare alders until I came across a thin stump, marked with the telltale grooves of beaver teeth. Alder shavings littered the ground. I wondered how recently this engineering beaver had been here, working on his or her house of saplings.

In the lace of branches before me, small finches began to congregate with chirps and flitters. A covey of little brown birds hopped curiously from branch to branch a few feet from my face. I felt like Snow White, friend of forest creatures. I held out my hand in invitation, hoping one might fulfill the fantasy and alight upon my finger. They declined, but fluttered around me with a chorus of chirps until, after what seemed like quite a stretch of time, they scampered off into the trees. I guessed that someone must have regularly fed them birdseed at this spot.

I later asked one of the women who lived at the retreat center if someone fed birds out by the beaver-chewed stump. She knew the spot I meant, rolling her eyes at the nuisance of beavers, but said no one fed birds that far from the house. I had been visited by the little flock for no other reason than to say hello. I was one with the land, connected with Spirit through her winged messengers. At the time, though, I did not yet know what message they carried.

I moved frequently as a child, my family always in search of cheaper rent or a shorter commute to work. One of our houses overlooked Washington's Skagit Bay to the west, and floated in a moat of blackberry brambles. Our nearest neighbor was two lots to the north; second-growth forest and a tangle of blackberries grew between us and her little lawn.

Across the street beckoned an empty lot, cleared of most of its timber but passable to adventurous eight-year-olds. Here I discovered some of my first spirit teachers: a circle of granite boulders. I named them Grandmother, Grandfather, Aunt, and Uncle, and played amidst their powerful energy beneath the draping branches of Douglas fir. I did not really know what *sacred* meant, but I felt a sweet and solemn power in this circle of boulders. To me, the needles padding the circle floor were made of magic. I would lean against the rough stones and whisper to them my secrets, flaking off bits of lichen with my fingernails. I felt them listening, felt the hum of their rock consciousness surround me.

These rocks, the blackberry brambles around my house, and the bay to the west taught me slowly and subtly how to listen to the land. From them I learned that a stone can have a personality, that the tides and sea weather affect the land, and that blackberry brambles bind and protect. The seasons of rain and sunshine, the prick of blackberry thorn, the call of frogs in a nearby stream—all of these taught me to pay attention while rooting me deeply in the language of the land. Of course, at the time, I didn't realize I was learning how to be a nature intuitive. I led a normal childhood, grew up, got married, and all that, but

I carried the teachings of nature in my body. Other life events helped to turn those teachings into the power to communicate with the land.

As a young woman, I grew interested in healing and energy work and studied Reiki and meditation. I developed my abilities to feel into people and situations through psychic attunement, weaving a keen energetic sensitivity with my nature lessons in paying attention. My nature path and my healing path slowly grew together like the brambles around my childhood house.

One afternoon, many years after I ran wild among the fir trees, my future husband and I explored the Washington Park Arboretum in Seattle, playing with the energy of trees. We rested our hands on their trunks and felt a spiral of energy pulsing sun-wise toward the sky. We wandered through the trees like wood nymphs until we happened upon a ring of thirty-foot-tall sequoias. As I stood in the center of the circle, my entire body hummed, as if I had drunk too much Seattle's Best Coffee. I inhaled deeply, and felt the moist soil beneath my feet, the stretch above of waxy green fronds, and the strength and vitality of these powerful trees. These sequoias share land with rhododendrons, ferns, and moss-infused grassy hills. In their midst one can hear traffic but can also sink into the ancient quiet of the waiting stones and the spreading green. The land around them, though cultivated, has its own wildness that has taken over the arboretum after many years of Pacific Northwest rains.

Without words, the tree spoke to me: "Let the flow of life carry you. The land supports you, cradles you, as it does us. You too carry water. You too breathe the air. We are one earth, yet made up of distinct organisms, each fulfilling our unique tasks as humans, as trees. Come spend time with us, learn to listen, and the flow of your life will unfold toward the highest good of all."

My ability to heal, to work with energy, and to listen to the land is the foundation for my life on earth. As a gardener, mother, friend, and writer, I incorporate my deeper understanding of the earth into all I do. While I can feel the pain of the earth more deeply than most, I can also understand the bigger picture. Hearing the voices of the trees puts life into perspective. Knowing the rhythm of a stone helps me slow down and tune in to a deeper wisdom that guides me through my life.

In what groves and valleys have you found your own teachers? The trees and stones, rivers and birds call to us: *Learn to listen.* An ancient relationship with plants and stones pulses in our blood like the wildness that reclaims cultivated lands, a relationship that can be rekindled even in a city or amidst suburban sprawl. When we slow down and tune into our subtle senses, we can find a whole new level of being, where plants talk and stones offer companionship. The world around us, whether a city lot or a stretch of protected wilderness, suddenly becomes alive in a whole new way. We find teachers and companions that help us learn what it means to live on the planet Earth.

What is your role on earth? Why are you here at this time? What is it that you seek as an embodied spirit? The answers to these questions can be found by awakening to the wisdom of the land. We begin by releasing some of our preconceived notions about the natural world.

Looking Deeply

This first exercise can be revisited whenever you need a new perspective. We begin here to help release perceptions of yourself, of your abilities to see and hear, and of nature. For this exercise, gather your journal and a pen, colored pencils, and a magnifying lens if you have one.

❧ Find a tree or bush outside or sit before a potted plant. First look at the plant without labeling or analyzing. Try to simply look, letting your mind be still. Notice the variations in color, the contours and shadows, and the shapes made by leaves, stems, bark, and so on.

Now open your journal to a blank page, and draw the plant without looking at the page. This is called a "blind contour drawing," and requires that you not lift your pen or pencil from the page. Do not look at your drawing as you go—keep your eyes on the plant. As your eyes follow the details of the plant, your pen follows on the page. The goal is not to create a perfect or even recognizable drawing, but to capture the essence of your subject while honing your skills of observation. When you have drawn one plant, do a few more blind contour drawings of different objects, such as a rock, blades of grass, or an opening flower.

The next activity uses a different part of your brain to sharpen your powers of observation. Find another natural object to observe, and on a fresh page, list every word that comes to mind as you look closely at this object. Look again, and keep writing. You may want to pick up the magnifying lens to get a closer view. Fill the page with words and phrases about this object. To give you an idea, read my own observation of a shell:

> Whorl point gradations white speckles on soft brown spiral lip shine stripes tiny hole purple gray sharp bumpy bit of dirt stripes of red scratches grooves sun-wise opening depth home expansion snail hollow little peak what happened there? worn beginning and end

Just keep going, looking deeper, touching if appropriate, even smelling, and keep writing.

Another activity to encourage you to look ever more deeply into the world around you is to free-write. This awakens the right brain. While outside, put your pen to the page and start writing down all of your observations (this time using full sentences if you like) of your surroundings. What do you hear? Smell? Feel on your skin? How does your body respond? Record your sensations and any emotions and memories that arise as you observe. Keep your pen moving. When you find yourself winding down, turn to face a different direction and keep writing. Or move to face the same spot from a different angle. Write until you have filled a page or two.

Now do the same thing, but draw. This time you can look at the page as you go. Do not worry about artistic merit, but keep looking more deeply. A big part of drawing is seeing what is really there, not what you think you see. Keep looking, and draw what you see.

Play with looking at the world as long as you like. Let your eyes open, see deeper, and allow Nature to speak to you. The land teaches us through experience. We find the true magic of the land first by being with Nature, allowing Her presence to speak to us through our senses and our own stillness.

❦

I learned from a friend that one of my favorite authors would be speaking at the local independent bookstore. I have long admired her as a writing mother, and I was then a new mom with my first book hot off the press. Her latest publication was about eating locally grown food, so I thought I might not only go see her and get my copy autographed, but give her a copy of my own newly published gardening book, *Sacred Land*. All day my stomach did flips as I imagined the moment when I would hand my first book to this esteemed author of five novels and four works of nonfiction. I was too nervous to eat dinner that night before driving off to the bookstore.

The boulevard on the way to the store is lined with maples. As I drove, I reached out energetically to the trees. They stood their stations, their roots mining deep into the clay earth in search of water, their spring leaves exchanging tree thoughts with the sky. In usual tree fashion, they rooted deeply without apology. Their trunks, spring leaves, and spreading branches fully expressed the ontology of treeness. I felt calmed by their solid presence. I would drive a block, my stomach knotting up, then stop at a light and chat with the trees. My stomach would calm, then I would breathe more deeply and drive on.

After the author's talk, I gave her a copy of my book. She thanked me, seemed interested in the book, and said she was pleased to have met me. I left inspired by her talk and her writing and did my best to let go of any outcome regarding my own book. But perhaps most importantly, I also carried with me the lesson of the trees to ground, center, and be still in the midst of life's emotional back flips. It reminded me of Eckhart Tolle's work. He writes,

> Presence is needed to become aware of the beauty, the majesty, the sacredness of nature. Have you ever gazed up into the infinity of space on a clear night, awestruck by the absolute stillness and inconceivable vastness of it? Have you listened, truly listened, to the sound of a mountain stream in the forest? . . . To become aware of such things, the mind needs to be still. You have to put down for a moment your

> personal baggage of problems, of past and future, as
> well as your knowledge; otherwise you will see but not
> see, hear but not hear. [1]

The Looking Deeply practices above, my visit with the finches, and my moments of calm with the maples are doorways into the present moment where we find the sacred. Being with nature allows us to really see, to still the personal problems, fears, and projections. In this present, still state, we are open to experiencing Nature as She really is, alive, conscious, and ready to reach out on a deep level.

Are you ready to enter the mystery school of the land? To see incarnate divinity all around? To find your life purpose and enter into a new way of seeing? Begin with the simple but profound practice of sitting in presence with the majesty of the earth. In the stillness that opens within, you will find teachers to guide you along your spiritual path. You will begin to understand the messages brought to you by birds and the wind.

That day in the wetland when the finches came to say hello, I knew something mystical had occurred, but I did not yet know what it was they came to say. Now, years later, I have developed my abilities as a nature psychic. I can look back to that afternoon and hear their message more clearly. It is the same message I share with you:

---

1. Tolle, *The Power of Now*, 80.

*You are on your right path. It is here in this moment that
you will find the answers you seek. Ground, settle into
yourself, and open to the possibilities the world has to share.
Slow down and resonate with the land. This is your purpose
as a human, yourself incarnate divinity. Welcome to the path
of Spirit.*

FURTHER EXPLORATION

Practice

As you move through your day, take note of the natural
world around you. Slow down and sit in presence with
house plants, trees at the side of the road, the wind as
the weather shifts. Begin to pay attention more deeply.
What happens in your body when you begin to see more
deeply?

Journaling

Write about your observations in your journal at the end
of each day. Describe your journey to work, playing in
the backyard with your children, and watching the sunset. You may wish to include in your journal an almanac
of your surroundings, such as where the moon is in her
monthly passage, what the weather brought today, and
what is growing in your garden or neighborhood. These
are all tools to help you see the world around you and begin to hear her messages.

Art as Meditation

Make an altar, a place to sit outside and be with yourself, write, and listen. This can be as simple as a special chair on your balcony, or a miniature temple carved out of your garden. Let yourself play by listening to the surrounding land and helping it to express its own sacred nature. Include your favorite colors, wind chimes, and anything that helps you feel joy and expansion. Consider the words of Madeleine L'Engle:

> My special place is a small brook in a green glade, a circle of quiet from which there is no visible sign of human beings. There's a natural stone bridge over the brook, and I sit there, dangling my legs and looking through the foliage at the sky reflected in the water, and things slowly come back into perspective. . . . The brook wanders through a tunnel of foliage, and the birds sing more sweetly there than anywhere else; or perhaps it is just that when I am at the brook I have time to be aware of them . . .[2]

---

2. L'Engle, *A Circle of Quiet*, 4.

two

RHYTHM OF THE BODY, RHYTHM OF THE LAND

It is summer, and the screen door has a way of being left open. My daughter toddles in and out of the
house, closing the screen only as a game. At the end of the
day, we have a flock of flies knocking against the windows
and dive-bombing our heads. I do my best to ignore them.
The meaty monsters who thwack against the light bulb, zip
past my face, and plop onto the wall finally provoke me to
roll up a newspaper and go hunting.

As soon as I contemplate flyocide, however, there is
chaos. One fly zooms crazy circles around the room, never
landing. Another goes still as a possum on the ceiling, out
of reach. A few more leave the room entirely. The flies
know I am about to start whacking them off.

I would think I was imagining things, except that every time my annoyance levels overcome my usual pacifism, the flies go berserk. They can tell I am about to go fly squashing. Do I transmit my thoughts on the field of all possibilities? Do tiny electrodes in my brain excite molecules in the air with the frequency of killing?

Cleve Backster, who studied the electromagnetic response of plants to stimuli in their environment, discovered that when living cells in the subject plants' environment died—including yogurt cultures and bacteria in a sink drain—the plants reacted with alarm.[1] Further studies determined that the plants and all other living beings live within electro-dynamic fields of energy.[2] These are the energetic molds that shape our bodies, and they extend into the world around us, connecting us with all other living things. When I decide to go on a fly-swatting spree, my stress level increases a notch as my endocrine glands release stress hormones into my nervous system, my palms get a little sweaty, and my heart rate increases. This minute stress response is transmitted to the flies via the electromagnetic field around my body, and they sense my change of intent. They react with understandable alarm in the same way Backster's plants reacted to the death of nearby living cells.

My connection to the field around me, from my emotions to the flies, is my body. My thoughts and emotions

---

1. Tompkins, *The Secret Life of Plants*, 11.
2. World Research Foundation, "The Electrical Patterns of Life."

release neuropeptides, chemicals that carry emotional messages throughout my body.[3] The chemicals exchange energy—charges and information—with the electro-dynamic field around me, and my state is felt by everything in that field. The labyrinth of these fields on a planet carrying almost seven billion people and potentially another thirty million or more species boggles the mind. Every time you think of something or take some action, however subtle, you affect a billion life forms. The electrical charges set off in your nervous system when you think, dream, move, or attend to something are what connect your mind with the world. Your physical body is your center in the world. It is the mast of your work as a psychic practitioner, tuning in to the radio signals of the earth.

In this chapter, we will explore the importance of tuning into your body for your psychic journey. Our body roots us here on earth while giving us tools to experience the Divine or Nature on an intuitive level. Your relationship with your body and your senses will affect your ability to attune with nonhuman and nonlocal (i.e., far away) beings. We cannot transcend our body until we fully inhabit it—and the healthy, full development of psychic sensitivities depends on your relationship with your body.

By consciously centering in the body, we can become more effective human beings, more aware of our impact on the world. We can enhance our awareness of our senses (which is what psychic ability really is) and actively

---

3. Pert, *Molecules of Emotion*, 275.

participate in the dance of energy all around us. For this reason, we can argue that your greatest magical tool is your body. Eckhart Tolle writes, "You are your body. The body that you can see and touch is only a thin illusory veil. Underneath it lies the invisible inner body, the doorway into being, into Life Unmanifested. Through the inner body, you are inseparably connected to this unmanifested One Life—birthless, deathless, eternally present. Through the inner body, you are forever one with God."[4]

The body is the gateway to your connection with Nature and the Divine. Psychic work, gardening, meditation, all rely on your body. Learning to pay attention to your body may be one of the most important skills you can learn in life, both from a physical health standpoint and from a spiritual growth standpoint. Attuning with Nature begins by centering in your body.

Western culture fears the body and fears being in tune with our bodies. Patriarchal religions (including capitalism) have taught us to ignore the body, suppress bodily urges, and sometimes punish ourselves for even having a body. The body has been regarded as sinful and dirty, something to transcend at death. From this attitude we have created a culture rife with eating disorders, chronic back pain, rape, and cosmetic surgery.

What kind of culture might we live in if the body were seen a part of the spirit, a divine expression, and a tool for our development? The sin is not the body, but in forget-

---

4. Tolle, *The Power of Now*, 96–97.

ting that the body is an expression of the Divine, rather than being the Divine itself. The body became sinful when people lost themselves in the power of the body and let it become God. When we *include* the body in our spiritual journey, without letting it take over and become the whole journey (as we do when using drugs or becoming addicted to sex), we find greater balance and harmony.

Your body is the one thing you carry with you throughout your life. Whatever your size, shape, and level of physical fitness, your body holds and expresses your spirit, your subconscious, and your mind. We are conditioned to think of the body as something we own and control (or over which we lose control); the mind as some sort of presence that resides in the brain; the subconscious as the hidden part of the mind (also generally part of the brain); and the spirit as an animating energy that goes on when we die and is housed *in* but is separate *from* the body. Begin to shift your thinking; the body is *all* of those things: an expression of your spirit, a tool for the mind, *and* a physical presence.

Somatic psychologists, those who heal the psyche through the body, know how deeply entwined the mind and body are; many see the body itself as your subconscious "mind." Biologists have found neurotransmitters and other molecules responsible for emotions throughout the body, not just in the brain.[5] Though "thoughts" get processed in the brain, the stimuli for those thoughts

---

5. Pert, *Molecules of Emotion*.

and our responses to them come from and are expressed by the rest of the body.

Your source of power begins in your body. You incarnated into a body in order to learn more about Spirit, and to grow as a Being. Jim Marion, a contemporary Christian mystic, writes that "The *only* way to enter the Kingdom of Heaven [unity with Spirit] is bodily. . . . Ascension into the nondual vision of the Kingdom of Heaven is the reason for the whole human enterprise God has created on this planet. *By means of our bodies* we somehow become gods. . . . By means of the polarities and dualities of space and time, we somehow transcend space and time forevermore."[6]

Our bodies carry us. They hold our consciousness as we know it. We must be able to inhabit our bodies fully to gain mastery over our consciousness. This is why so many mystical practices use the body as a tool, as in yoga and sitting or walking meditations. The body is contained in or infused with the spirit; to reach the spirit, we go through the body.

Just as you took time to find presence with Nature through seeing, you can find the sacred by sitting in full presence with your own body. This is known as sitting meditation. Sitting meditation deepens us into our center, the body, and brings us into Spirit through that center. It deepens our awareness of being in a body, including our senses and our energy. It is from this center and this

---

6. Marion, *Putting On the Mind of Christ*, 211.

actively felt sense that we can learn to attune to nature. Our foundation practice of awakening and attuning is sitting meditation.

SITTING MEDITATION

The practice of Buddhist-based sitting meditation brings us into the present moment through the body. It is similar to the observation exercises in the previous chapter, but instead of watching something outside yourself, you watch your own body. The body is the tool for becoming present and connecting with your spirit.

❧ BEGIN BY SITTING upright on a meditation cushion or other supportive cushion that allows your knees to be lower than your hips, so that your vertebrae can stack comfortably. If you find it uncomfortable to sit cross-legged on the floor, try sitting in a chair with a small pillow under your spine. Set a timer for ten or fifteen minutes to start; you may decide on longer meditations in the future, but fifteen minutes can feel surprisingly like an eternity. You may choose to rest an open-eyed, soft gaze a few feet in front of you or close your eyes. Each choice presents a different challenge to your attention. Either way, focus your attention on your breath and your body. Notice your breathing pattern without trying to alter your breath. Notice areas of tension. Your thoughts will swim past, occasionally pulling you under and distracting your attention. Name this "thinking," and return to your breath.

Watching your breath and noticing when you get lost in thought, then noticing your return to awareness, are meant to be very gentle practices. Pema Chodron writes, "Touch the breath and let it go," then, "When thoughts come up, touch them very lightly, like a feather touching a bubble. Let the whole thing be soft and gentle, but at the same time precise."[7]

Sit for fifteen minutes witnessing yourself, noticing your thoughts, any difficulties being gentle with yourself, and so on. The goal is presence: spending time with yourself, your body, your mind. Cultivating your awareness of the Witness, the part of you that is beyond ego and simply *is*, witnessing all, is an important part of psychic awareness. You must be able to slip into witnessing to differentiate what is *you* and what is *other*. Witnessing yourself is also an important tool for learning to face, feel, and process challenging or overwhelming emotions. These strong feelings, such as love, anger, anxiety, and so on, come up in the normal flow of life, but they can also arise while feeling into other consciousnesses. When you can sit with strong sensations, you will know what is too much and when to back off. You can face more intense emotions without becoming

---

7. Chodron, *The Wisdom of No Escape*, 17–18.

overwhelmed or shut down. You can also fully own your emotions, so you do not project them onto others. Finally, you can understand what is your "stuff" and what belongs to the person or being you are communing with.

I go into the Witness as a starting point for reaching out to other beings. I calm, settle into my Witness, then expand my awareness into a tree or a stone or a client who has come to me for healing. Sitting meditation is one way to cultivate your awareness of the Witness. Your skills as a nature intuitive will grow from there.

GROUNDING IN THE BODY

Sitting meditation is about presence and being. Use it as your foundation for the work in this book and your work as a spiritual practitioner. While the guided meditations and practices offered here help you focus the mind and develop skills such as psychic attunement with trees and stones, do not neglect the practice of simple sitting meditation. Awareness of yourself and the ability to focus are invaluable tools for psychic awakening. Sitting meditation grounds you in your own body and in the present moment.

After sitting meditation, you will likely feel grounded and peaceful, but you may find that the more directed meditations found in this book, as well as other trance work, can leave you feeling a little checked out. Taking a few moments after these meditations to practice simple sitting can help you return to your body, grounding in yourself. You can also use Starhawk's technique "Anchoring to Core Self" found in her book *The Earth Path*:

> ❧ BEGIN BY SITTING in a comfortable and safe place, and envision the situation in which you feel most at peace, most yourself. Then say to yourself the name you most identify with, and notice where this name resonates in your body. Choose a posture or gesture that feels connected to this sense of resonance and relaxation. Find an image that represents these feelings, and a word that typifies this sense of home base for you. Whenever you say this word, do this gesture, and picture this image, you will return to your home, anchored state.[8]

I find this exercise useful in times of stress as well as after going into trance states, like meditating or communicating with the natural world. We cannot operate effectively in the world if we are not fully grounded. Take time to ground in the body and on the earth before proceeding.

THE ROOT OF PSYCHIC DEVELOPMENT

What we call "psychic awareness" is actually using the heart center and other non-logical sensory tools to pick up information around you and listening to that information with heightened senses. We pick up the subtle

---

8. Starhawk, *The Earth Path*, 63.

energies around us by synchronizing with them through the body, especially through the heart. The electromagnetic field produced by the heart extends beyond our body, attuning with the information it encounters. Stephen Harrod Buhner writes:

> The heart is not only concerned with its interior world. Its electromagnetic field allows it to touch the dynamic, electromagnetic fields created by other living organisms and to exchange energy. . . . The heart not only transmits field pulses of electromagnetic energy, it also receives them, like a radio in a car. And like a radio, it is able to decode the information embedded within the electromagnetic fields it senses. It is, in fact, an organ of perception.[9]

"Extra-sensory perceptions" are not *extra* so much as *extended.* We learn to extend our awareness into the fields around us through our heart and other electromagnetic fields. We extend the sensitivity of our senses, which can sometimes lead to hypersensitivity. I can be hypersensitive to noise, for instance. I need quiet to think, write, or sleep. My daughter, a very perceptive child, is easily overwhelmed by wind, loud noises, or bright sunlight. Many psychic people find they are ultrasensitive because they have such a highly differentiated nervous (i.e., electrical) system. Conversely, practices that hone your physical senses of sight, hearing, touch, taste, smell, and proprioception strengthen your psychic abilities—and help you

---

9. Buhner, *The Secret Teachings of Plants*, 88.

avoid overstimulation by encouraging mindful awareness of sensory input.

Paying attention to the body and its nervous system will bring you gradually and safely into psychic consciousness. I know I am moving too fast with my psychic or subtle development when my sensitivity to stimuli is a little too overwhelming. When I feel too easily overcome by noise, touch, or visual images, I take time to ground in my physical body. By rooting in my core body, I am able to handle the world, including both physical stimuli and psychic information.

I will explore psychic development further in future chapters, but for now, let us focus on how the body and your bodily senses are the tools of psychic development. The first step to seeing this natural awakening of the extended senses is to pay attention to what you are sensing right now.

❧ GATHER THE FOLLOWING: a raisin, a jar of cinnamon, a feather, and a chime or small bell. Ground and center. Survey the items before you with your eyes, as you did in the previous chapter with a plant. Look, then look again. Write about what you see: the wrinkled raisin, the sweep of feather, the exact shade of cinnamon, the light on the metal chime.

Now breathe in the scent of cinnamon. Describe it as best you can. What does it remind you of? Can you distinguish different scents within the spicy bouquet? Take a little pinch of the spice in your fingers and roll it around. What is the exact texture?

Put the raisin on your tongue and chew slowly, really noticing every tiny sensation in your mouth as you eat this dried grape. Notice what your muscles do in order to swallow. Is there a trace of cinnamon on your fingers? Taste that.

Brush the feather against your skin. Try to describe how it feels. Play with different pressures, different parts of your body—how much more sensitive are your lips than your arm?

Ring the chime or bell a few times, really paying attention to the exact resonance. What happens in your body when you ring the chime? How does it feel to listen?

Notice the sensation in your body of *paying attention to something.* Feel how you subtly lean toward whatever you attend to, as if your skin reaches out just a little to your object of attention. Notice how shifting your attention shifts sensation in your body. This is the same sensation you cultivate as a psychic; your awareness shifts toward people or things outside of your body through the bodily practice of attention.

Take a moment now to soak in all these sensations. Ask yourself: *Who is aware?*

You are your body; your inner body and your sensation both—and you are something greater, some being beyond the manifestation of these processes. Sit for ten minutes in awareness of your inner self. This is your soul. Notice your soul's relationship with your body. *Who is aware?*

The body roots us in space and time. It is our bridge between the soul and the world. As intuitives who seek an authentic connection with the natural world, we must take back the body as a sacred temple and powerful tool. It is our *sacre corps*, the sacred center of all we do. Before doing psychic, healing, or spiritually based work, ground and center in your body. Pay attention to your sensations and to the manifest world. Begin here, at home in your own sacred temple. From this place, we can walk the path toward a mystical relationship with nature.

FURTHER EXPLORATION

Practice

To deepen your ability to attune with nature, spend time in meditation, and in sensing your body. Go for a walk in a favorite place, letting your attention settle into your body and the land around you. Stretch your body, dance, or play with different textures from nature on your face, hands, arms, and feet. Hold in the awareness that your body and nature are expressions of Spirit. Meditate on the idea of *expression* while playing outside.

Take moments throughout your day to feel your body. Notice how the feeling in your body changes as you interact with different people, circumstances, and environments. Ask yourself the following questions:

Where do you carry emotions? You might, for instance, hold anger in your jaw. When an emotion arises, in what area of your body do you notice new sensation?

Where do you notice muscle tension? You may hold emotions chronically, often as muscle tension. Is your chest tight, your breathing restricted, or your stomach clenched? Just begin to notice and see what unfolds. There is no judgment here, only noticing. It may take a while to grow into body awareness—keep witnessing and noticing what happens in your body, and let a new relationship with your body unfold.

Do any memories arise as you tune in to different parts of your body? Memories always surface when I get a massage and the therapist works on certain parts of my body. Sometimes I know why a memory surfaces, other times I do not. When you pay attention to various areas of your body, what images, emotions, and memories surface on their own?

How does your body feel when sitting near your favorite tree? When making love? When cooking dinner? When arguing with a friend? Since spirituality is about experience and noticing what is, include witnessing how you feel in your body during different experiences as part of your spiritual practice.

Journaling

Take some time every day to journal about what you notice in your body. Write about your meditations and about your discoveries as you tune in to your body. What does your body feel in this moment? How does that change when you are around stones, water, and trees? What might this teach you about attuning with the Goddess and the land? Try to find language for the unique and varied sensations always occurring in your body in response to each day's experiences.

Art as Meditation

Another way to witness the body and how we use it to carry our experiences is through art. On a large piece of paper, have a friend trace your body, or draw a rough outline of your body from memory. Ground and center. Fill in the body outline with colors or pictures from magazines that represent how each part of your body feels, or how you feel about that body part. Spend some time on this project, maybe going back to it a couple of times. You may wish to share your Body Map with a trusted friend when you are finished. Discuss or write about what you discover about your body and your relationship with it.

This kind of body-centered work can bring up strong emotions, especially if you have a history of body trauma, such as abuse or injury. If deep or troubling emotions arise, I strongly recommend finding a good body-centered psychotherapist or art therapist who can support your journey of inhabiting your body. For referrals, try the United States Association for Body Psychotherapy, http://www.usabp.org; the American Art Therapy Association, http://www.arttherapy.org, 1-888-290-0878; and the International Expressive Arts Therapy Association, http://www.ieata.org, 1-415-522-8959. Also ask friends who have therapists they like, call local social service agencies for referrals, or ask your employer's human resources office for a list of suggested therapists.

three

TUNING THE
INNER EAR

When my husband and I were looking to buy a home, I had two requirements for our house: garden space and lots of trees. Finding a home shaded by trees can be something of a challenge in the suburbs of Denver, especially in our price range. I rejected house after house simply by looking at pictures online—no trees, no trees, no trees.

Then we found a rare gem: a three-bedroom house, twenty minutes from downtown, nestled among five mature trees and three scraggly junipers. Shortly after we moved in, I sat down to get to know our miniature forest. I grounded and centered, following my breath. I reached out to each of the trees, my energy brushing against them like an invisible feather. Then I took them all into my field of awareness, feeling them surround the house. Their roots extended deep into the packed clay earth, cradling our little house in a subterranean hammock.

Through their leaves, the trees took in the breath of the neighborhood, connecting to every tree and plant for miles around through water vapor and carbon dioxide. Their roots wove a spider-web network with all other trees, supporting the land and exchanging nutrients and knowledge. My energy expanded farther, slipping along this web like drops of dew. In my mind's eye I saw the green world-wide web, the sheath of trees and shrubs that wraps the earth in living embrace. I sat for a few moments, breathing trees. I gave thanks to all the trees of the earth, and to those who shaded our own roof. I pulled my energy back into my body, grounded, and returned to everyday awareness.

As humans, we exist in space and time but we also possess the power to meld into other times and places. Using the tools of our subtle senses, we can slip into streams of awareness different from our own, communicating directly with trees, stones, and other non-humans. We can connect with the living net of plants connected around the globe; or with the fold of rocks and soil beneath our feet; or with the living potion of water, the akashic record of the earth.

When I reached out to the trees, I moved into subtle vibration with them, entraining with their energy. Entrainment is where two vibrations of different speed, like the classic example of the ticking clock pendulums, move into synchrony over time by being near each other. Physicists believe it has to do with an energy exchange between the differing vibrations. One clock gives the other clock packets of energy that speed it up or slow it down. They become equal, attuned together.[1]

Psychic attunement with a person, plant, or other being relies on the entrainment of energies. This can be as simple as feeling calm around a calm person, or borrowing a little energy from a tree to be able to communicate as a tree. Obviously when you chat with a tree (or another human), you do not give each other so much energy that you become an amalgamation of each other; you just share enough energy to be able to communicate on some level. Shamans who study shifting energies in great detail over many years may develop the ability to morph so completely that they shape shift into another being, but most of us develop the capacity to attune only slightly.

Since humans and trees and rocks are a whole symphony of vibrations, it is hard to say exactly which vibrations entrain, but perhaps we may think of the entire symphonies getting a little bit synchronized. Were we less complicated, like the ticking clock pendulums, we would become each other more easily. But there is a reason I am a human, my cat is a cat, and finches are finches. There is a reason we retain our ontological identity (what that reason is exactly has become the great question of religion and philosophy, so I am not going to attempt to answer it,

---

1. Davy, "In Sync," *Current Science*: 10–12.

except to say that our individual beingness is central to our spiritual growth).

While the cells of my body are spending time as a human, they do not immediately become tree or river. However, energy does not operate by the same rules as does matter (otherwise known as slowed-down energy, per the theory of relativity). Energy can slip free of space and time. I can use my energy, the rapid vibrations of awareness that extend beyond me, to feel into the tree by becoming just a little bit of a tree. I can tap into the continuum of all things and become a little bit "not me." As the saying goes about walking a mile in someone else's shoes, when you spend a few moments in the skin of a tree, you gain immense knowledge about being a tree. You learn more about nature, the land, and about the spirit of the land.

Psychic awareness of other states and beings is a natural process of human development; it's a matter of learning to feel the language of the heart as it entrains with the energies moving around and through us.

Psychic "powers" are rather like playing concert piano. If you cannot play piano, you can hardly imagine what it might be like to be up on stage, your fingers caressing the keys with beauty and skill. You shake your head in wonder that someone can do such a thing. But if you dedicate yourself to a practice, over time you could potentially become skilled at playing the piano, or communicating with plants, or writing poems. Like playing piano, developing your psychic awareness is a matter of time, personal development, and (to some degree) a natural aptitude. Learning to listen to your "inner ear" requires patience and dedication.

Ken Wilber explains that there are *states* of consciousness, like a peak experience, and *stages* of development. You can move through natural developmental stages more quickly if you visit associated states more frequently. For instance, when you meditate regularly, you accelerate your mental and spiritual development, and will reach a higher level of evolution faster than if you never meditated.[2] Attuning your subtle senses is the same. Spend time opening to plant, stone, or river consciousnesses, and over time it will become part of who you are. Just as a concert pianist cannot imagine *not* having the ability to play piano, over time you will naturally be able to attune with the energies of other beings and think little of it.

LEARNING TO ATTUNE

When I studied cello in college, I found the best way for me to learn a song was to listen to a recording with sheet music in front of me, then play along with the recording while simultaneously reading the music. I was terrible at knowing the name of a note on the page, but I could find that note with my ear and my fingers. My husband, a professional musician, learned to play his saxophone a little differently: his mathematical brain quickly took in the patterns of notes on the page, and he learns a song

---

2. Wilber, *Integral Spirituality*, 87.

through the actual notes, which he can then find by name on his horn.

We all learn skills differently, depending on how our brain works. Whether you are trying to play an instrument or deepening your ability to "listen" psychically, you will have a preferred way of learning. We take in information and process it (i.e., learn) aurally, visually, and kinesthetically. People have a preferred order of learning through these styles. For instance, I like to see something, then hear information about it, then do it. When I do a physical action, I have it forever, but it takes me a little while to get comfortable with that action. Physical activity can be overwhelming to me, but once I get comfortable with an action, I am quite skilled at it, such as driving, riding a bike, or dancing. Friends of mine are the opposite. They need to jump right in and try something, then look back at what they did and talk about it. Other people talk and listen, then go through the movements, then watch someone or see it in their mind's eye. Whatever you prefer to do *last*—feel it, hear it, or see it—and whichever style feels the most vulnerable but the deepest may indicate your preferred psychic style, or your unconscious learning channel.

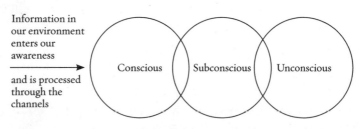

The Learning Process

When I learned about the unconscious learning channel, it helped me not only to understand how I learn (and why physical activity can be so overwhelming), but also to understand my intuitive style. I am clairsentient, meaning I *feel* a bodily sense when picking up psychic information. That information is then translated into words and images. Psychic information goes the opposite direction of conscious learning. Instead of coming in through our conscious awareness and being filtered through to the subconscious and unconscious, it enters our body-mind through the unconscious and is filtered up into the subconscious and conscious levels.

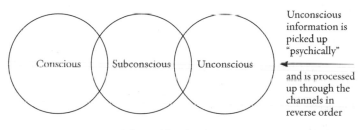

Unconscious information is picked up "psychically" and is processed up through the channels in reverse order

The Intuitive Listening Process

You may feel, see, or hear intuitive information. None of these is better or "more psychic," although as you gain more advanced psychic abilities, you will likely incorporate more styles. More of your nervous system will be able to pick up initial information or process the information picked up by the electromagnetic field of the heart and sense organs. You may also have moments of feeling or hearing when usually you see non-manifest levels—again these are the stages and states Wilber talks about. For now, though, you will likely have one preferred mode of picking up intuitive information.

It can be freeing to realize your own intuitive style. When I realized I "hear" energy as a *felt sense*, I was better able to work with my own psychic abilities. When you realize you see, hear, or feel intuitive information, it will be easier for you to trust and develop that ability. The best way to develop your psychic sense, as with any other skill, is to use it, and you cannot really use it until you know what kind of skill you have, whether you predominantly see, hear, or sense things. Then you know what sort of input you are looking for and can give it your full attention.

If you are interested in exploring more about learning styles as discussed here, I highly recommend any of Dawna Markova's books, such as *The Art of the Possible* and *How Your Child Is Smart*.

PLAYING WITH PLANTS

While the focus of this book is on talking to nature, your psychic intuition applies to reading all sorts of beings, including "natural" elements and human beings. Of course, it is all nature. What you choose to feel into, talk with, and learn from depends on your interests. I am a gardener, and I grew up in rural or suburban areas. I taught environmental education to sixth-graders when I was in college. The natural world is dear to my heart and endlessly interesting, so I call myself a nature intuitive or nature psychic.

Nature is also a good place to hone your skills as a psychic because you don't need to find human subjects to practice on. Plants, stones, and water tend to be more forgiving, more open, and more readily available. They are much less judgmental. The only challenge in learning to talk to plants is that their feedback comes in a different language than we are used to speaking. The process of becoming a nature intuitive is all about opening to new channels of noticing. Through these channels, you will get responses and feedback from the natural beings you chat with.

I find it easiest to begin with plants. They are not as complex as bodies of water and are "more conscious," if you will, than rocks. Their vibrations are closer to that of humans than the mineral world, but not as complex as animals. We begin our practice as a nature psychic by chatting with a single plant.

The first plant I intentionally and consciously conversed with was a garden pea. I sat in front of the curling tendrils of a pea plant and asked if I might chat with her. I felt a sense of *yes* come over my body. I grounded, softened my physical vision, and shifted my awareness into the plant. I felt warmth, light, and joy. The pea welcomed me to a new world of talking with plants. She was delighted I had begun with her.

I was able to communicate with the pea plant the first time I sat down because I had for many years spent time with plants, meditated, practiced Reiki, and engaged in other practices that opened my subtle channels. Since then I have incorporated subtle communication into my daily life, my gardening, and my work as a healer and writer. Over time it has gotten easier—and I still have a lot of room to grow as I evolve spiritually.

I offer the following practice to you wherever you are on your path of intuitive discovery. Whether you are just beginning to tune in to subtle energies or have been working as a spiritual practitioner or healer for years, this is a simple way to begin to talk to the natural world.

❧ WHEN YOU HAVE a few moments to yourself and will not be interrupted, practice tuning in to plant energy. Choose a plant you would like to connect with, perhaps a favorite flower in your garden or a house plant you encounter daily. Sit in a comfortable position near this plant, and take a moment to ground by feeling your energetic roots reach deep into the earth below. When you feel a heavy sensation in your lower body, almost as if you have grown physical roots, you are grounded. Take a few breaths while you sense this.

Bring your attention more deeply into your body. Release muscle tension throughout your face and body, and follow your breath for a few moments. When you feel centered and grounded, ask the plant in front of you if you might have a chat (you can do this in your mind or aloud). You will be extending your energy into the plant, and vice versa, so asking permission is an important step.

If the plant tells you *no* through an image, a felt sense, or a word, choose another plant to work with. For instance, when a plant, animal, or person does not want to be felt into psychically, I get the sensation of a solid wall between me and their invisible inner self. I feel blocked from them. When they are open to me, I feel a melting sensation, like I can enter into their space. Most plants will welcome you in; nature is always communing with other beings via electromagnetic impulses and is quite ready for psychically awakening humans to say hello.

When you get a welcoming response, extend your energy into the plant by extending your focus into the plant and the area around her. It's kind of like when you are aware of another person entering the room. Tiny electrical impulses on your skin turn toward him as he enters, and your senses tune in to his movements, his mood, and so on. Your energy reaches for him. Reach your attention to the plant, crossing the space between you to entrain with this plant.

Bring your attention into the plant. Say hello, and pause a moment to see what you get back. You may get words as a response, aloud or in your mind. You may see images or get a feeling. Play around with what you see, hear, or feel.

Spend a few moments chatting with the plant, sensing energy and allowing the experience to flow over you, and then give thanks and pull your energy back into yourself. If the plant asked you for water or fertilizer or a new spot, respond accordingly. Then go get a cup of tea, stretch, and feel the inside of your body to come back fully to yourself. Anchor to your core. You have been in a trance state, which can leave you vulnerable to others' energies. Take the time to return fully to waking consciousness. After your encounter with the plant, record your experience in your journal or by painting or draw-ing. Creating a tangible memory of your psychic communication helps you reflect on the experience, making it real.

FURTHER EXPLORATION

Practice

Try meditating with a tree. Choose a favorite tree in your yard, in a nearby park, or on your way to work. Ground and center. Reach out to the tree with your energy and, if you wish, your hands. Our hands are often particularly sensitive to energy, especially if you practice healing work or another meditative act using your hands, such as sculpting. Let your energy connect with the tree, and ask it in your mind if it is open to working with you energetically.

Once you are welcome to proceed, feel into the tree. Entrain with the tree. Feel how her roots stretch deep into the soil while her branches reach high into the sky. Feel water and sap moving inside the trunk. Feel worms squiggling around her roots. Notice areas that feel dead. Notice the feel of the sunlight on the tree's bark and leaves.

When you are finished exploring and getting to know the tree, pull your energy back into your body. Feel your breath, your heartbeat, and the sensation of being inside your body. Remain fully inside yourself and look at the tree. How has your experience changed your perception of this tree or trees in general?

Journaling

Write in your journal about your psychic experiences with trees and plants. How do you pick up psychic information? Were there some trees or plants that felt more comfortable to you? Did some ask you not to attune with them? Could you sense why?

Write about how living with plants and stones and rivers as individuals might affect you and how you might live your life differently.

Art as Meditation

Make a collage or drawing that you can use in meditation to help align your energies with plant spirits. Tear out favorite pictures of trees, flowers, and other plants from magazines and glue them to a piece of cardstock or construction paper in a mandala[3] or other pleasing arrangement. Or draw your own images, perhaps from your time communicating with plants. Place your art in a spot you see daily, or where you meditate, do ritual, or write in your journal.

---

3. "Mandala: Circle. A symbolic representation of the universe that is visualized to enhance spiritual practices." Koda, *Sacred Path of Reiki*, 245.

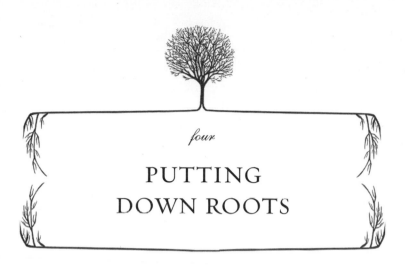

four

PUTTING
DOWN ROOTS

One very rainy November, my daughter, husband and I visited my parents in Olympia, Washington. It turned out to be the wettest month on record. Despite the cold damp—the kind that permeates two shirts, a sweater, and a rain coat to soak deep into your bones— I desperately wanted to spend some time on a nearby beach. We waited for one of the rare and precious breaks in the constant downpour and drove ten minutes to a beach-front park. I prayed we would have at least half an hour to stare at the waves, pick up slick, salty stones, and reconnect with my alma mater, the Puget Sound.

We were, of course, the only people there. It was Thanksgiving Day, and most people sanely preferred to huddle around a fireplace and a roasting turkey than pick their way carefully across a slippery, stone-covered beach. But here we were, feeling thankful to be at the shore, albeit beneath blackening skies. I pulled my hood tight around my face against the biting wind. While my husband taught our two-year-old daughter the ancient art of throwing rocks into the water, I took a moment to reconnect with the choppy Puget Sound. I reached my energy out into the bay, the southern point of the Sound, and let my awareness creep north, past Seattle, along the San Juan Islands, and up into the wind-tossed Strait of Juan de Fuca that divides British Columbia from Washington State. I could feel the heavy roll of orca whales, the slip of boneless giant octopus, and the shift of salmon heading back to sea.

It was like a hug that brings tears to your eyes, a return to the place where you are most yourself. The swirling tides rushed around me, embracing me. I felt recognized. Which is not to say that the water actually recognized me, but that the feeling in my body was the same as when you meet a kindred spirit and see the connection and recognition in another person's eyes.

I must have lived in the Pacific Northwest during some of my past lives. In this life, I was nearly born on a ferry between West Seattle and Vashon Island. My family moved frequently, but stayed close to Puget Sound. The Skagit Valley with its migrating snow geese and rich, black farm soil, the sparkle of sunlight on Seattle's Elliot Bay, the presence of the divine mountains Baker and Rainier; the land around the Sound is a part of my body and my soul.

Shortly after college I met the man I knew I wanted to spend my life with, and we moved to Colorado so he could attend graduate school. We ended up staying for a once-in-a-lifetime job, buying our first and then second houses, and having a baby. I learned to live at the base of the Rocky Mountains instead of at the feet of Mount Baker. I adjusted to high-altitude cooking and temperature variations. But I am like a selchie, the seal woman who leaves her watery home to live on dry land. Before I moved to Colorado, I drew a card from Philip and Stephanie Carr-Gomm's *The Druid Animal Oracle*. I drew Seal, who teaches about love, longing, and dilemma. "The Seal speaks of the longing of the heart," I read, "although the Seal may represent loneliness and separation, a selchie imprisoned on dry land, remember that the time will come when she will be released and will act as a guide and companion through the watery realm of the emotions and the Underworld."[1]

In Colorado I learned to garden in a completely different climate than my native Seattle. I volunteered at a farm. I practiced healing work at a nearby spa, which I walked to daily. By spending time in this foreign climate, I learned to listen to the land I now call home. Here I learned how to interact with the land in ways I might not have in Washington. The Sound and the cracked, dry mountains teach different lessons. Here I learn about stone and earth. I learn about dry wind and thunderstorms. My mind as well as my

1. Carr-Gomm, *The Druid Animal Oracle*, 147.

soul learned from this land, for I took classes at Naropa University, which was built in Boulder because (I have heard) of the intense power of the land to encourage work on one's karma. Whether or not this story is true, Naropa would certainly be a different school were it located in Seattle rather than in Boulder. Having attended most of my schooling in Washington, I know the differences well— differences due partly to the energy of the land itself.

In one of our first Colorado homes, we lived near a hiking trail that snakes into the foothills. The trails can go from slick mud after a drenching rain to dried clay, cracked from wind and sunlight. One dry summer day, I headed up the steep trail near our house. My shoes gripped the hard, dried earth as I breathed heavily. A raven flew overhead, her raucous *haghhh* greeting me. We were in the midst of a drought. I took a moment to ask the land about dryness.

I grounded, then reached my awareness out into the packed clay and shrubby, windblown trees. I felt the recent summer dryness and the ten-year drought as a larger pattern. I saw a bigger picture than the human perspective and understood the drought to be a response to great planetary shifts. Individual trees or even whole forests might dry up and die, but the land itself knew this was part of a longer stretch. It was one land made up of individual trees and stones, but one land working as a complex individual responding to the greater environment.

I began to see how the land is a living network of which I am a part. Though I can plan, dream, write, and grow spiritually, I am a part of the land around me, just like the raven and the sage brush. For the first part of my life, that land community was the Pacific Northwest. More recently, my network has been the Rocky Mountains. While I do not always eat local food and have never worn clothing made from fibers grown near my home, the cells of my body and the weft of my spirit are interwoven with the surrounding land. Who I am is deeply tied to the land. I am of the Pacific Northwest and Puget Sound, but I am also, now, of the Rocky Mountains at the edge of the Great Plains.

You are an individual in the web of your environment. Your body, your center, radiates your own signature energy out into the land around you. You absorb the energy of the particular trees, stones, and waterways that make up your home. You attune to the vibrations of the land itself. Any home you have lived in has affected your resonance, and how we interact with our home affects our relationship with the land and Spirit.

THERE'S NO PLACE LIKE HOME

Take a moment to get to know the land on which you live. Attune energetically with the earth to feel its own unique magic and begin understand how it affects you. The energy of the land will partly determine what lessons you learn during each phase of your life. Even the moment-to-moment forces on the land, like weather, affect you. Become used to attuning to your environment by using the following meditation.

❧ SIT AT THE base of a tree or large rock near your house, and take a few moments to breathe. Feel the pressure of your sitting bones on the ground. Feel the air shifting around you. Take in the sounds of birds, cars, planes, animals. Ground and center. Ask the land permission to connect. You will most likely get a positive response.

Reach your energy out into the soil beneath you. What do you see or feel? Tree roots? Rocks? Underground rivers? Let yourself play, not worrying about whether or not you are right about what is underground. Notice how your body reacts to the land as you synchronize with its energy. Allow yourself to become a piece of the land, plants, stones. Release a little of your humanness and feel what it is to be the land. After ten minutes, pull your energy back into your body. Anchor to your core self.

Try this exercise daily or as often as possible, even for a few minutes. Over time, let your awareness broaden to include a greater area of earth. Include the air, trees, rocks, and even homes around you (being careful not pry into the energies of your neighbors). Ask the land to teach you about itself. Ask it if it has anything to tell you. Practice the meditation in different places as well. Try connecting to the land in the city, in a park, in wilderness, and even inside your home or office. Record in your journal what you see, feel, and hear.

The land around you is your church, and your temple, when you follow a spiritual path tied to the earth. The land, trees, rivers, and rocks speak sermons about life and death. They offer guidance for how to live in harmony with the seasons. They can teach you also about the greater web of life, for they live within it more consciously than we do. Your own personal energy sings with the energy of the land to create a unique spiritual path that is about the here and now. For this reason, no one person's path is the same as another's—and yet if we all tied our spiritual growth to the earth (for why else would we be on this planet at this time?), we would find a common understanding amidst a symphony of spirits.

As a part of finding your center and learning to listen to the Goddess, take some time to notice how your land and any other homes where you have lived have affected who you are today. Consider the following questions:

- Where were you born?
- Where did you grow up? How was your schooling shaped by the land?
- Where did you choose to go when you became an adult? Why?
- How have places you traveled affected you? Consider the weather, modes of transportation, and culture that is shaped by the land, and so on.
- Where would you love to travel or vacation? Where would you love to live? What about the land draws you there?

- How do the seasons unfold where you live? How do you interact with them? Do you have a favorite season?

- What other cycles affect your land, such as drought, bird migrations, the jet stream, etc.? Can you see aspects of these in yourself? In this time of your life?

- When you spend time in nature, where do you go? Why? How do you feel while there and upon returning home?

- How do your house and yard or patio reflect your personality? Why did you choose your current house or apartment?

- How are your job, profession, and schooling shaped by the land around you?

Explore the answers to these questions, and any thoughts that arise as you contemplate home, in your journal. Give yourself time to think, coming back to the questions over several days. Your subconscious and dreaming minds will mull over the meaning and significance of your homes past and present, and writing will help mine these hidden thoughts as well as record your conscious ideas and memories.

ASTROLOGY AND ELEMENTAL ALCHEMY

Alchemists believed the world was made of four earthly elements: earth, air, fire, and water. The four elements

can still be used as metaphor to understand the relationships among energies. Different spots on the planet, like
individual people, exhibit more of the qualities of some
elements and less of others. The Pacific Northwest, for
instance, is very watery, while the Rocky Mountain region
corresponds more to earth energy. You, too, have a certain makeup of elemental energy in your body and spirit,
often exhibited by your astrological horoscope. How your
elemental energy interacts with the elemental energy
of the land determines some of the lessons you will face
while living in that location.

The basic idea of astrology and astrocartography is that,
at the time of your birth, Earth was in a certain spot in its
rotation in relationship to the Sun. The zodiac—the great
circle of the Sun as it seems to revolve around the Earth—is
divided into twelve "houses" named after constellations.[2]
When you say you have Libra in the fourth house or your
Sun is in Aquarius, it means that at the time of your birth,
these signs and planets appeared to be in one section of the
zodiac as seen from planet Earth. These energies working together reflect your personality, lessons you are here to
learn, and even aspects of your past lives. Astrocartography also looks at where these energies fell on Earth at the
time of your birth, and therefore where on Earth certain
energies are strongest. For instance, the line of Neptune falls
right over the West Coast in my chart, so I tend to be more

---

2. Parker, *Parker's Astrology*, 18.

dreamy and psychic when on the West Coast. It is a very watery place for me.

What are the elements of your own land? What about in your own personality and body type? Here are a few elemental correspondences.[3]

EARTH
Direction: North
Nature: Soil, mountains
Time: Night, winter
Qualities: Body, creativity, fertility, strength and groundedness
Animals: Bear, wolf, horse
Zodiac signs: Virgo, Capricorn, Taurus

AIR
Direction: East
Nature: Wind
Time: Dawn, spring
Qualities: The mind, imagination, intelligence, intuition, inspiration, music, and communication
Animals: Birds, flying insects
Zodiac signs: Gemini, Libra, Aquarius

FIRE
Direction: South
Nature: Sun
Time: Midday, summer

---

3. Curott, *Witch Crafting*, 78.

Qualities: Will and energy, passion, courage, determination, drive, desire, and power
Animals: Cats, dragons, phoenix
Zodiac signs: Aries, Sagittarius, Leo

WATER
Direction: West
Nature: Oceans, rivers, and rain
Time: Sunset, fall
Qualities: Emotions, love, dreams, compassion, and playfulness
Animals: Dolphins, fish, whales
Zodiac signs: Cancer, Scorpio, Pisces

Llewellyn's astrological service is a reliable source for astrology charts of all kinds. They can be reached at 1-800-THE-MOON (800-843-6666) or online at http.//astrology.llewellyn.com/ For a good local astrologer, you may ask natural-healing practitioners and your friends for referrals.

Psychic Relationship with the Elements

You can also attune psychically with a place to see how it interacts with your energy, whether it's the place you now live, a place you lived in the past during a difficult time of life, or a place to which you consider moving. Use the "There's No Place Like Home" meditation, but take it a step further by feeling into the qualities you notice and analyzing their significance. Also observe how those qualities affect you emotionally.

❧ I AM A watery, airy person living in a fiery, earthy land. This balances me out but can also feel tiring at times. How does your elemental energy interact with the dynamics of your home? What do you notice as you extend your energy into larger spheres, from your house to your neighborhood, to the city, and beyond? When you look at yourself as a dot of energy living in this spot on the planet, what do you notice? What does it mean that you are in this spot on the global web? Spend some time exploring these ideas to begin to identify more clearly your role in the world as it is reflected in the land.

FORCES OF THE LAND

The "nonliving" forces of the land include mountains, rivers, canyons, lakes, and other natural bodies. These forces affect the energy of the land, shaping the way we move through the land and how we feel. In Seattle, for instance, the long and narrow city bustles between a mountain range and a labyrinthine body of water. Volcanic mountains Baker and Rainier keep watch over the city. These natural gods, or land spirits—water and mountains—affect the weather, the way people drive (traffic slows to a crawl when the seemingly perpetual clouds rise and Rainier stands at her full glory, towering nearly three miles above Interstate 5), commerce, and one's energy. Waterways are especially powerful, shaping the earth energetically as well as literally.

"Wherever there is water, life can become active in the material world," wrote Theodore Schwenk.[4] Water shapes and informs the material world in many ways. Land nourished solely by underground aquifers looks and operates differently than land fed by a whitewater river. Human, plant, and animal activity on land is also shaped by the type, quantity, and energy of water. By learning more about the water that serves you in your home, you can understand more about the land around you.

When you turn on the tap in your home, where has that water been? Do you drink water from your watershed or is it piped to you from another region? The water I drink in Denver comes from a combination of aquifers and the South Platte River, filled largely by rain and snow hitting the western slopes of the Rocky Mountains. The aquifers on the eastern side of the mountains are made of alluvial silt, which is formed over time from river sediment. The South Platte River flows right through the city. Water absorbs aspects of everything it contacts, and I absorb the water when I drink or bathe in it. Through my water, I take in the energy of mountain rivers, clay silt, and the city of Denver. I drink aspen, clay, and grassland.

The bodies of water nearest to my house are human-made runoff and overflow drains. I live within walking distance of Westerly Creek, an algae-covered, garbage-littered corridor designed to enhance water surface drainage. The lives of the people who live here reflect the rather human-

---

4. Schwenk, *Sensitive Chaos*, 98.

engineered energy of the land. I live in a working-class neighborhood, in a city dedicated to *doing*: real estate, biosciences, aerospace technology, and other human-focused industries make the money in Denver. How the land is shaped and what kinds of waterways helped shape that land reflect the energy and lessons of the place.

Your watershed links you with every other person, animal, plant network, and industry that also exists in that watershed. Wes Jackson argues in his essay "Toward a Common Covenant" that in order to heal the damage we humans have done on earth in seeking to meet our needs and desires, we must find a way to understand the earth, rethink the way we grow our food, and see the truth of our interrelationship with the planet. One way we can begin to accomplish these goals is to unite with others in our own watershed. He writes, "The river will always speak a language that humans can learn with a little effort—a language in every way local, in every way universal, but in no way foreign."[5] By listening to the river that gives us water, we learn about direct relationship with the land. We learn about the interconnection of ecosystems and human activity. We learn about what it means to inhabit a home.

With a trip to the library or a quick search online, you can learn more about your watershed, the body of water that ends up in your plumbing. Research a little about that water: how it gets to your house, if it is underground

---

5. Jackson, *Altars of Unhewn Stone*, 157.

or above ground, and the minerals or pollutants in the water. Consider what this information says about your city, home, and this time in your life. Is your water trucked in from far away? Do you drink a lot of bottled water? Do you live closer to salt water or large bodies of fresh water? Write and dream about how these energies affect you and your life.

♣ MEDITATE WITH THE water around you, attuning with it psychically. This meditation can be done sitting in your house, or even while you soak in the bath. Ground and center, breathing into the earth. Reach your awareness into your home's plumbing. Follow the pipes out of the house, first reaching into the water's source, then following it as it leaves your home. Where does it go? What energies does it absorb from the land around you?

Now reach out to the nearest body of water, be it a drainage or irrigation ditch, a pond or lake, a river, or the sea. Notice how this water forms the land, how it makes life possible in your manifest world. Ask it what you are here to learn, what it has to teach you about life.

Give thanks to the water, and come back into your body. Spend some time feeling the inside of your body so you don't float away with any water sprites.

Mountain Mama

I ask the Rocky Mountains: "What would you like me to tell the world about communicating with mountains?"

I see the myriad habitats, the complex synchronization of rock and plant matter, the pockets of water and weather that make up a mountain range or even a single mountain. I feel the density of clay, aspen wood, and rock. I feel the weight of waiting stone, sitting in time in one shape, fluid in geologic time. Millions of years ago, this land was as flat as the plains to the east. Then rocks rose from the core of the earth to form mountains, which were carved by glaciers and erosion. One day these mountains will fold back into the earth, or crumble to dust from eons of wind and rain. They are solid and dense, but only by my human terms.

Within these mountains live animals and plants who have responded to the requirements of altitude, sun, rainfall, and other environmental influences. They are formed of the mountain, and to the mountain they will return. As with most other life on earth, these living beings spend a tiny pocket of time competing for energy from the sun, then passing their energy onto other beings, and so on until the end of an ecosystem.

You are a part of this unfolding as well. How the mountains, valleys, rivers, lakes, and other forces near you came to be will influence your own energy. What do the these nature gods have to tell you about life and home? How do they influence your life? What are the lessons these beings have to offer? And what have you to offer them?

Journal about your home and how it ties you to the earth. Only by understanding what it means to call a place home can we learn to live in harmony with the earth.

FURTHER EXPLORATION

Practice

Plant a tree. Find a spot where you can put down roots, in your backyard, in the corner of a wild park, or in a friend's yard near your own. Find a small seedling native to your area at a local nursery or tree farm (very small ones are often inexpensive, and you can even find them free at Arbor Day or Earth Day festivals). Or, if you have room, purchase a fruit tree or other tree for your home. Following the instructions that come with your tree, plant it, and water it. Place your hands on the soil around the base of the tree, sending green-white energy into the earth and the tree (above and below ground). Ask the tree to help you learn the meaning of roots, and of being grounded. Let a part of you settle into this land. Talk to the tree and ask it about its experience of living in this spot. Care for this tree as it grows. If you move from your home, say goodbye and thank you. A part of you will always live in this spot. Write about how this experience feels to you.

Journaling

In addition to the journal activities in this chapter, write the story of home. What does *home* mean to you? Where do you feel most at home? The planet is our temporary home, but to live most fully and in balance, we need to live each day respecting her as our home. How does your awareness shift when you see your current house and city as home? When you see the planet as home?

Art as Meditation

Gather stones, pinecones, shells, or other objects near your home that represent the land around you and your connection with it (ask permission from the land to remove the objects). Collect a few personal items—a strand of your hair, an old earring, or a little totem animal from a bead shop or toy store. Glue these items into a shadow box, or put them in a jar or small box. Decorate the frame, jar, or box with images or colors that say *home* to you. Set your piece on your altar, mantel, or dresser where you can see it. Let it be a totem of home, a symbol of your current connection with this place.

five

THE NATURE
OF HOME

After I graduated from college, I moved back in with my parents. They and my high-school-age brother lived in a two-bedroom duplex. Though I did my best to keep my influence and belongings to one corner of my brother's room, it was a tight fit and something of an imposition on the poor guy. I didn't yet have the funds to move out on my own and didn't know anyone who might be a good roommate, so I took it upon myself to find the whole family a new house.

I found the rental quickly, a four-bedroom with a large basement for boomerang college grads. Our only problem was we were short about a grand on the deposit. I put it out to the universe that we needed this house. A week later, my dad received a check in the mail for almost three thousand dollars from a class-action suit he forgot he had taken part in. We moved the day after Christmas.

At the time, I had just started a new job at an acupuncture school that was also preparing for a major move. Like my family, the school had outgrown its cozy location and needed several thousand additional square feet. Three moving trucks would be rolling up a few days before New Year's to pack up the entire school and move it a few miles away. At the new location, I would also be getting a new title, moving up from receptionist to financial aid administrator.

While all around me my walls were shifting, I was falling in love with a coworker. I was pretty certain it was another typical-me go-nowhere crush, but try as I might, my feelings would not go away. My new position at the school meant that I would have a more flexible lunch break, since I was no longer tied to the front-desk phones, and this coworker and I started taking long lunches. We planned a joint birthday party, as our birthdays were one day (and ten years) apart. I still wasn't expecting anything.

However, with a little prayer and a bit of love voodoo, I crafted an altar in the love and romance corner of my new bedroom. In feng shui, each corner of a room, house, or property signifies a certain energy. The far right corner from the front door is about partnership and love. In this corner of my room, I placed a vibrant plant, little hearts, and pictures of paired animals. I felt a little silly, but the idea of not moving this relationship to the next level was just unthinkable. This coworker had been told by an astrologer that he had already met the woman he would one day partner with, that she had brown eyes and a lovely voice, and that he would start dating her in February or March. When he told me this, I thought, *It will either be me or some amazing woman I will hate.* I dusted the love corner, brought in fresh flowers, and tried to stay open to any outcome.

Our birthdays came, a party with all of our closest friends at a gourmet vegetarian restaurant. We had been lunching together now for a month and a half but had not otherwise seen each other outside of work. A friend who came to the party said, smiling slyly, that it felt like a wedding reception. My crush and I sat next to each other as the guests of honor. For the first time, I reached for his leg under the table. He took me home that night, and we kissed for the first time. We made plans to spend my birthday together, carefully avoiding mention of it being Valentine's Day. When he dropped me off, I went to my love and romance corner and gave thanks to the universe and to this new home for helping me to transform the energy in my life.

SPIRIT OF THE HOME

We tend to think of our homes as separate from nature, but in reality, *everything* is nature. Machaelle Small Wright channels Nature in her book *Co-Creative Science*. At one point, Nature says, "Nature is the consciousness that comprises all forms on all levels and dimensions. It is form's order, organization, and life vitality."[1] In other words, nature is the translation of Spirit into matter. Therefore, everything with form is nature: the book you are holding, the chair beneath you, the air you breathe, and the walls or trees all around. Your home is one aspect of nature, and of your relationship with the natural world or the planet that makes your home possible. Your house or apartment is your home base, where you live in constant communication with the universe through intention and awareness.

Beneath form (or inside and through form) is energy. Form is the manifest solid that energy creates through its rapid movement and specific intention. It is this energy, this consciousness that nature translates from the causal level—the realm of Spirit—that you interact with when you reach your attention into another form. That form can be a tree, a person, a cat, or your house. In effect, you touch the spirit of the tree, cat, person, or house. The spirit of your house is its energy, a matrix of form (the walls), history, and use (how the furniture is arranged, the daily energy of people in the home).

You have probably entered spaces where your felt instantly comfortable, and others that left you feeling itchy and cold. The energy of a space is created by many vibrations, from energy in the earth beneath a building to the history of its inhabitants to the intention that went into its construction. All of these factors taken together create

---

1. Wright, *Co-Creative Science*, 4.

a sort of House Spirit. While we usually think of a house as "not natural" and outside as "natural," one who is in tune with her environment and the energy of the land includes human-constructed environments in her awareness.

I find it makes a difference in how I feel in my home when I get to know the spirit of the house. I feel this spirit or energy automatically, but when I take time to attune with and communicate with that energy, I feel more comfortable, grounded, and safe in my home. Here is a meditation to get to know the spirit of your home.

❧ SIT IN A comfortable spot in your house where you will not be interrupted. Ground and center by paying attention to your breath and the weight of your body on the floor or chair. Send roots into the earth beneath you. Settle into your body in this space and time. Let go of thoughts as they arise, and come back to your breath or heartbeat.

Shift your awareness to the walls around you and the floor below. Notice the ceiling above your head. Say hello to your house. Reach out your attention into the consciousness that resides inside the energy of your home. Each home has its own personality— feel into the individual that is your home. What do you sense about this House Spirit? Do you feel welcome? Afraid? Tense? Peaceful? Do any images or phrases arise?

Thank the building for sheltering you. Tell your House Spirit what you dream for your home. For instance, I want my home to be a safe space that feels peaceful and full of joy. I want family members and guests to feel welcome and loved. I want the kitchen and dining areas to host many joyful dinner parties where we serve local, organic, gourmet food. I want laughter to fill the house. I want my daughter to be happy and safe under this roof. What do you dream of? Ask if there is anything your home needs in order to fully reflect these desires.

Send your awareness through the house to feel for any stuck energy. This feels like indigestion or congestion, and it can be caused by clutter, poor decorating or furniture placement, strangely shaped spaces, and history. If a trauma occurred in your home, while you lived there or previously, you may feel it as stuck or cold energy. Note those areas; we will clear them later.

Sit for a while just feeling the energy of your house. How does it reflect your energy and that of your family or housemates? How does it not fit?

Thank the house again, and pull your energy back into your own body. Ground and breathe for a few moments. Write about your discoveries in your journal.

HOME AS A MIRROR

The home is a mirror of our inner house, and it likewise reflects what we project onto the world. Our relation-ship with the home, the body, and the manifest world all reflect upon each other like the facets of a diamond.

When a person feels at home in her body, her home, and on the earth, she cares for all three. She moves with grace, drawing to her the life she desires. On the other hand, one who has a trashed and cluttered house, a crappy yard, and a poorly attended self lives a frustrated and stagnant life.

Attending to any of these manifest mirrors affects the others. Care for your body, and suddenly you feel the need for a healthy home to house that body. Care for your home with mindfulness and attention, and your relationship with the world changes. You have a safe home base. You want to see cleanliness, beauty, and care in the world outside your home as well. Care for the body, earth, and home develop naturally when a person attunes regularly and authentically with the earth. The spirit is fed through authentic relationship with the land, and upon the foundation of right relationship with spirit and earth grows a healthy life, including a clean and happy home.

See the nest of concentric circles: spirit in the middle, surrounded by body, then home, then local environment and community, then the planet, then Spirit. They are interconnected. Drop a rock into the center of this pond of connected circles, and see the ripples affect the whole.

One practice that ripples through these relationships is intuitive connection with nature—outside the home, and within it. As nature is all things, the translation of Spirit into matter, your home is an expression of Spirit and of your spirit. Care of the home then becomes a contemplative and spiritual practice, where we meet our connection with Spirit through Nature and the home. Everything that occurs in the home can be a practice of spiritual attunement. These especially include food, clothing, and your home environment.

Food

Water, air, and food cycle from the earth through our bodies and back into the earth. Our food brings with it all it encountered as it grew: sunlight, chemicals, minerals in soil and water, vibrations of the road it traveled upon, attention from the farmer, and so on. What kind of food you purchase affects what energy you bring into your home and body. Local, organic, seasonal food has a cleaner, more full vibration than a listless and anemic tomato harvested in January and shipped thousands of miles to a refrigerated grocery store (refrigeration itself sucks flavor from a tomato). Mindfully grown, harvested, and transported food brings mindfulness into the kitchen and your body.

Then you prepare the food. Even a quick meal can be cooked with attention and care. Give thanks to noodles as you drop them in a pot of boiling water. Chop up some locally grown greens and an onion. Toss an onion in olive oil, picturing the olive groves beneath a dry, hot sun. Drain the pasta, with thanks to the water and fire that cooked your processed grains, and toss the whole mess together with a prayer for health and joy. Grate a bit of locally made Parmesan, and present the meal to your family and friends. Light a candle, take a moment to pause for reflection and thanks, and dig in!

I love the description Barbara Kingsolver gives of Italians eating. "Watching Italians eat (especially men, I have to say) is a form of tourism the books don't tell you about. They close their eyes, raise their eyebrows into accent marks, and make sounds of acute appreciation. It's fairly sexy."[2] It's also good for their health. Eating slowly and with joy improves digestion and prevents overeating. Taking joy in your food sends a message to your body that you are safe and supported, and that the food is healthful and good. It also sends a message of thanks to the earth, both in your energy and in the leftovers as you give them back to be cleansed and recycled. Kingsolver points out that Italians keep their slim figures by eating small amounts that they fully enjoy. Mealtimes become a social meditation in this way.

Clothing and Accessories

When you arise in the morning, notice any natural fibers in your sheets and blankets. If you sleep in pajamas or a gown, these, too, probably contain some cotton or silk. The clothes you wear each day often contain natural fibers like cotton, hemp, and silk. Most of our modern clothes contain a blend of natural and synthetic fibers. Of course, synthetic fibers are made from nature as well, for all is nature. All is Spirit translated into form.

---

2. Kingsolver, *Animal, Vegetable, Miracle*, 247.

On a morning when you have a little time to muse, attune with your clothing, bedding, napkins, and other fabrics you encounter. Come into the witnessing mind, and reach your attention into the fibers of fabric just as you did with a plant or tree in the last chapter. Can you sense where it came from? If it was sprayed with chemicals? What the silk worms or cotton plants experienced? While some of your sensations will surely give you real information about your clothing, more importantly this exercise asserts the far-reaching affects our choices and behaviors have on the planet, and how dependent we are on the plants and animals of the earth. You may be surprised at what arises in your consciousness.

Your jewelry also comes from the earth. Sadly, many mining practices cause pollution or rely on dangerous manual labor. Gold, for instance, is usually extracted with cyanide, which leaks into water, killing fish and wildlife and contaminating drinking water.[3] Diamond mining disrupts local ecosystems, especially soil (the foundation of all life in a given area) and nearby rivers. There is a strong link between diamond mines, civil war, and human-rights abuses like child labor and extrajudicial executions.[4] Look for environmentally friendly, fair-trade certified jewelry when purchasing new. Stick to hand-made beads, hemp, and silver or gold made from scrap metals. Buy from local artisans. Any jewelry you have now, cleanse by soaking

3. Ban Cyanide! "Gold Campaign," Rainforest Information Centre.
4. Amnesty International, "Democratic Republic of Congo."

in salt water overnight (if this is safe for that particular type of gemstone) or smudging with smoke. Give thanks to the earth for its gift and to the people who harvested and crafted your jewels.

Cleaning the Home

There are many natural, nonpolluting cleaning products available at your local natural food store, but you can also make your own cleaning potions with a few simple ingredients. White distilled vinegar mixed with equal parts water will clean almost anything. For clearing out drains or cleaning the bathtub, mix a half cup of vinegar with a few tablespoons of baking soda. Pour it down the drain, followed by boiling water. In the tub, wipe out with vinegar, then with soda. Rinse. Polish furniture (test on an inconspicuous place first) with equal parts olive oil and vinegar. Throw some white vinegar in your wash water or during the rinse cycle to remove spots and deodorize. For more ideas, see The Vinegar Institute's page "Uses and Tips," http://www.versatilevinegar.org/usesandtips.html.

For a deeper clean, awaken the power of a "spring cleaning" by attuning in meditation with the vinegar, water, baking soda, and other natural cleansers. Ask these natural ingredients to help dissolve unwanted, outdated energies while they scrub away the grime. To keep your house from smelling like salad dressing, fill a spray bottle with distilled water and a few drops of your favorite essential oil. Lavender, rosemary, and frankincense are my favorites.

❧

Clearing the clutter in your home clears clutter in all areas of your life, as all is connected. A cluttered area is difficult to navigate and offers opportunities to lose objects or ignore business. It reflects a cluttered mind and life. Organizing your house, getting rid of extra junk, and cleaning a space all help you clear your mind, literally put your affairs in order, and move with greater freedom. The metaphorical and literal implications for clearing a space mirror each other and can be worked with for great effect. My experience with the love corner of my room in my parents' home is an example of how our space mirrors our energy and the energy of our world: by clearing a space in my room for romance, I cleared a space in my psyche, and possibilities opened up.

You change the flow of energy through the house by moving furniture to improve daily flow (like being able to walk through the living room without knocking your knee on the coffee table), deflecting unwanted or stuck energies with mirrors, and bringing in desirable energy with plants, water, and chimes. Before you can start shifting energies around, however, you need to start with a clean space.

Take a day or two to clear your space, or if clutter is a real problem for you, designate a month or longer to declutter. Recycle old magazines, throw out the extras in the junk drawer, donate clothes you never wear, recycle or shred files you no longer need to hang on to. Keep only what you love, use, or that has real sentimental value. Get rid of the rest. If packratitis is a major issue for you, enlist the help of a trusted friend or even a therapist to help you weed through your stuff.

For more thoughts and ideas on clearing out clutter, see Cindy Glovinsky's *Making Peace with the Things in Your Life: Why Your Papers, Books, Clothes, and Other Possessions Keep Overwhelming You and What to Do About It* (St. Martin's Griffin, 2002).

Next, go back to any of the areas that came up in your meditation with your house as feeling congested or just off. If an area feels stuck, stand in that space and reach out your intuitive awareness into the room. What feels sticky, like mud? What would happen if you shifted the furniture around a little? How does a new configuration change how a space feels? Play with differing weights of objects, like large heavy furniture and tall or dark objects versus smaller, airier pieces. Leave some space around each object. Leave window areas clear if possible, and make sure doors can open freely.

If a space feels stuck, try freewriting. Sit in a space and ask it what is wrong. Then write anything and everything that comes to mind. Ask the space what happened here that makes it feel stuck or heavy. Ask it what it needs. Ask yourself what your dreams are for the space. Write without editing, and see what comes up. If you are an auditory psychic, this might be a powerful way to get unconscious intuitive information to surface.

If you are still stumped by a space, turn to the Chinese wisdom of feng shui. The phrase means *wind water*, and it is all about the flow of energy through a space, indoor or outdoor. Feng shui operates on a series of rules based on Chinese astrology and energetic metaphor. To examine the energy of a space and its metaphor in your life, apply the *ba gua*, or energy map, used in feng shui. Each corner, from the perspective of the front door, represents an area in your life, like the love and partnership corner I worked with after college to find my special man.

FRONT DOOR

Of course, while the work on the outside is important and real—like putting two red candles in the love corner—it must be paired with internal work. Meditating in your space on each subject and asking the house spirits for guidance will bring you closer to manifesting your dreams from the inside out. Placing plants or wind chimes in stuck areas helps to move energy and can be startlingly powerful, but things can only come into your life when you are open to their gifts. If I hadn't been ready for a long-term partnership, no feng shui or special potions would have manifested my marriage.

Feng shui is a vast discipline, much of which is outside the scope of this book, but if you are interested in perusing it further, I recommend the following books:

- *Creating Sacred Space With Feng Shui: Learn the Art of Space Clearing and Bring New Energy into Your Life* by Karen Kingston (Broadway, 1997)
- *Feng Shui Step by Step: Arranging Your Home for Health and Happiness—with Personalized Astrological Charts* by T. Raphael Simons (Three Rivers Press, 1996)
- *Feng Shui for Beginners: Successful Living by Design* by Richard Webster (Llewellyn, 2002)

HOME: IN AND OUT

As nature intuitives, we feel clearer and more grounded when surrounded by green and growing things. Your house, clothes, food, and furniture are all part of nature, but they can feel a little stuck without the enlivening sparkle of plants and other unaltered natural products. Go for a smooth flow from your indoor home to the outside by blurring the edges of what is in and what is out. Let nature spill inward and create living spaces outside.

Here are a few ideas for blurring the edges between the indoors and out.

- Include potted plants, either flowers or herbs or both, directly outside your door—this works especially well with a glass door, but any doorway benefits from the continuity of plants. Keep the eye moving from the outside inward by putting a few of the same plants, or similarly colored flowers, right inside the door. If you struggle with transitions in your life, greening up your home's threshold may help.

- Let vines explore the room by draping them on furniture, over archways, and across windows. Screw little hooks into the wall for them to grow across. Choose a vine that does not cling to walls, as does ivy. Pothos vine (*Epipremnum aureum*) is a popular choice.

- Create a little rock garden or terrarium in a glass bowl or fish tank. Choose your favorite ecosystem, like a temperate rain forest or a sandy beach, and re-create it in miniature. For a long time I had a miniature Pacific Northwest in a terrarium in my office. I included stones, shells and sand dollars from the beach near my parents' house (removed with the permission of those objects), and a small fern. The back of the terrarium was a collage of images from the Pacific Northwest. This little

PNW altar helped me, ironically, to come to terms with living in the Rocky Mountains.

- Display shells, rocks, pine cones, and other natural objects on a mantel or bookshelf. I have heard that people who do this naturally are probably angels in disguise.

- Place a tabletop fountain in a visible spot. The money corner—the back left corner of your space from the front door—is an especially auspicious place for flowing water.

- Attach bird feeders to your windows, so birds come right up close to snack. Keep a bird book handy for identification, or attune with them in meditation.

- Use natural, chemical-free materials throughout your home, like sisal, bamboo, cork, and sustainably harvested wood. Not only are these better for the planet, a green home feels more solid and comfortable, especially for the energetically sensitive person.

Bring your nature awareness into your home by attuning regularly with your plants, stones, shells, and even the building materials. You will be more aware of the spirit of the home, and the home will reflect your spiritual energy. Even people who do not consider themselves intuitives will notice the difference. Most visitors to my modest but mindfully attended home comment on how peaceful and comfortable my house feels. I suspect the effect is not due solely to my smashing interior design.

FURTHER EXPLORATION

Practice

Perform a house blessing. You may want to choose a special day like May Day to bless and cleanse your house, but you could choose any time your home needs refreshing. First clean the house and clear up clutter. Then infuse a bowl of water with a little salt and some rosemary essential oil, which purifies and protects. Say a prayer or chant over the water, sending divine energy into the water with your hands and intention. Starting at the front door, walk in a clockwise direction through your house. Sprinkle some of the water in each corner, asking for blessings and clearing out unwanted energy. If this is a holy day, a new house, or if you've had a particularly challenging time in your life, go through the house again, clapping three times in each corner to break up extra sticky energy. Finish with a third sweep, this time with a little incense—sustainably harvested sage or sweet grass. The smoke will help cleanse the corners while bringing your prayers into the spirit realm.

Journaling

Write a letter to your house. Tell it all your dreams for remodeling, for your life, and for its care. You may want to do this once a month or a few times a year, noticing how your relationship with this crafted space changes over time.

Art as Meditation

Craft an item to bless and cleanse, such as a wind chime or Brigit's Cross. A simple chime can be made out of craft glass, shells, little pieces of bamboo, or even old spoons. Wearing safety goggles, drill holes through shells or spoons, or use hot glue and a glue gun to attach fishing line to your objects. Tie them to two dowels, tied together to form an X. Hang near the front door or in a corner that needs improved energy movement.

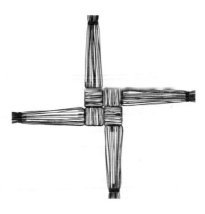

To make a Brigit's Cross, gather at least nine twelve-inch-long strands of wheat or grass. Historically these were pulled rather than cut. Soak in water to soften, and gather four rubber bands or string to secure the ends. Remove your straw from its bath. Hold two straws vertical, and wrap one around the other at the center to the right, making a sideways *T*-shape. Hold the center tightly and rotate the whole thing ninety degrees counterclockwise. Add another straw, and wrap it around the vertical straw, as in the first step. Repeat the turning and wrapping until you have used all your straw pieces, then secure the ends.[5]

Traditionally the Brigit's Cross is hung over the door on February 1 or 2, Brigit's Day, or at the beginning of spring. Each spring, a new Cross heralds the new returning green.

---

5. Amber K, *Candlemas*, 68–69.

six

CULTIVATING GREEN RELATIONSHIP

*I*n Anne McCaffrey's fantasy world of Pern, dragonriders "impress" telepathic dragons, linking their minds and hearts with the great animals as they hatch from dragon-sized eggs. The human riders and their dragons share thoughts and emotions and form a lifelong team trained to fight the planet's deadly threat, a flesh-eating spore from space.

Reading about impression at the dragon's hatching brings tears to my eyes. I used to dream of having such a companion, a compassionate and intelligent beast who knew my heart inside and out. Together we would share our secrets and loves, and we would fight passionately to protect the world we so deeply cherish.

Today I have such a dragon. Instead of scales and faceted eyes, though, my telepathic companion is made of green and growing things: peas, beets, and onions. Her heart is made of worms and compost. She is my garden.

I attune regularly with my garden. In pushing my fingers into the soil, I settle into an ancient rhythm. I feel a deep peace and a sense of belonging and home. I am the architect, and the land carries out my plans. I listen, and the land teaches me about stewardship and cooperation. It mirrors my inner processes and ties me deeply to my home.

When I first moved into the house I currently inhabit, the lawn was mostly packed clay and scraggly weeds. I sat down with the land and told her my dream: a large garden that could supply my family with at least half our food; room for my unborn baby to play and grow; dinner parties on the patio lit by a twinkling of tiny white lights; a pond; herbs; a bird sanctuary (despite my cats); a home to nourish deep roots for my heart and soul. I ordered nine cubic yards of mulch from the city, free from the forestry division as long as I accepted the entire truckload. They dumped it in the driveway with a great cloud of dust, commenting on my pregnant status. With only three months to go before the birth of my baby, I slowly moved mulch to the corners of the lawn and garden paths. I pulled weeds (resting to give my belly room to breathe) and started a compost pile. When I spotted the neighbors mowing the lawn, I waddled over to beg their bags of clippings. They looked at me like I was surely a crazy person but handed over the black plastic bags to the wacko pregnant lady.

I double-dug the beds, a technique to loosen soil with minimal disturbance of microbe populations. It was slow going, requiring frequent breaks for my baby-growing self. But I was a driven woman, nesting in the most basic sense of the word. I constructed a cold frame out of scrap wood and planted kale, lettuces, mâche, and carrots. I put my hands on the soil, sending the soil and the seeds green-white energy. I put my hands on my belly, feeling the feisty child inside shift under their warmth. This was the soil that would nourish my child. Here I would teach her about the balance of the land to give and recycle life, to nurture and grow and, in time, sink back into itself.

While I dug and sculpted, one wheelbarrow or compost pile at a time, I talked to the land. I asked for her advice. Where should the cold frame go? What could I plant this fall before the freeze came, usually around Halloween? Should a path go here? What is needed for better drainage? I received images and bodily senses in reply. My subconscious and the land itself worked in tandem to offer kernels of dream images: plant here, dig there, build here. We became a team, the garden and I. Our mission to create a haven for my family, healing a neglected plot of land in the process, slowly progressed through our joint efforts and intentions.

The plot of land had been sorely neglected in the past. The trees were hacked at with a chainsaw, weeds were left to take over, and the packed soil grew spindly grass.

I slowly nursed the land to health by working with it to landscape and cultivate. I am not a big fan of lawns, but I kept little patches that we attend with aeration and organic fertilizer. A chemically treated lawn feels a lot like an overzealous salesman that has eaten one too many pork pies; I wanted my lawn to feel peaceful, even if it turns yellow in July. Grass turns brown in heat to protect itself; forcing your lawn to be green creates imbalance in the land. I didn't plan to go totally native, and I do water my smaller patches of lawn in early summer, but beyond that I tried to trust the urges of the clay soil to let my bits of lawn be the grassland it is.

The garden has taught me about manifestation. Having very little lawn, I needed more grass for my compost, so I asked the landlord of the vacant house next door for his grass clippings. He brought me ten bags of the stuff every other week, grass from both of their rentals. I needed more mulch and some help spreading it; mulch was free from the city, and friends were all too happy to help. I wanted boards for my raised beds and an old window for the cold frame; a neighbor who works in construction gave me two-by-fours for the beds, and we replaced a shoddy sliding glass door on our house, using the old door for the cold frame. With few resources besides my determination and what I believe was influence from the spirits of the land, I crafted a magical garden of herbs, flowers, and vegetables out of almost nothing.

Now the land and I are a part of each other. Literally, for I eat the food she grows and pour my moonblood on the compost. But we are also connected energetically, in the way of McCaffrey's dragons. Through our work and our chats, the garden and I have impressed each other, meaning we have fused our hearts to work as a team. When I am feeling spread too thin, the garden does poorly. When I slow down and sit in stillness in my yard, she shows me new ideas, new perspectives, and we both thrive. As I write, I stare out the office window at a box elder that looks like it's dying, while I am simultaneously shedding a part of myself. I am building a career and raising a toddler, and as I steward a new life, my old self dies away. One of my beds is doing poorly this year, and the garden told me it needed a season of rest to further break down the soil. I myself have been, to use a dear friend's phrase, going like banana cakes, and I too need a season of rest before I can grow anything else. I'm letting the bed sit and looking forward to some rest for myself this fall. I will buy organic vegetables from the farmers' market and get some from a farm share rather than tending them myself. This summer, I am growing more words than tomatoes, and the garden seems to agree that it's for the best.

When I need peace of mind, I go dig beds and turn the compost. Caring for my friend puts things right. Garden chores settle me into my core, watering my own roots while I water the beans. I breathe the trees' breath, walk upon the worms' ceiling, and press my hands into the decaying soil. I make love to the garden, and our relationship deepens.

The gardener is an active participant with the land. As we explored previously, you are a part of the land. Your home affects who you are. The garden is a microcosm of this relationship, a place where you can see your effect on the land and taste its influence on you. It is also a place where you give back to your home and to the land. Your own energy, hearth, and intentions for health and wholeness become woven through the soil beneath your feet and the food you place on the table. Gardening is a practical act of stewardship that says to the land, "I honor our relationship. I am a part of you, and you of me. I will care for you, and you for me. Blessed be."

In the pumpkin patch, you grow more than gourds; you also cultivate a deep relationship with the earth. A garden practice is as important to the spiritual earth-path as meditation or ritual. It is a direct line to the earth, a mini-representation of our relationship with the land as humans, the architects and engineers of the natural world. In the garden you learn about the natural cycles of life and death, and about the complex and lovely interconnections among all things. Your garden—whether a planter box of herbs or a six-acre plot—is where you learn to speak the language of the earth.

When you place a seed in the soil, you plant your heart in the earth. A part of your own energy is left with that seed, nourishing and shaping it along with soil nutrients, water, and sunlight. Your kitchen waste and your time and attention become food for the plants. The energy of the earth in turn shapes you; the plants become food for your family. The garden is all about give and take, a sharing of energy. Even spending time in the garden or gazing upon flowers grown in your own yard shapes you as you entrain with the energy of the land. We are all of the earth, but people who garden consciously participate in this exchange.

Gardening is another form of meditation. It can be a time to enter into stillness as your body works. You listen to the birds, discover worms in the soil, and watch green buds break free from their winter sleep. These all serve as reminders to open to the miracle of the planet. You breathe more deeply, exchange energy with the land, and settle into your body. Here you return quite literally to your roots as an animal who relies on the soil beneath your toes as provider and home.

CULTIVATING INTEGRITY

"[Agriculture] dominates the global land mass so completely because we have used our *unspecialized* and versatile capabilities . . . to meet our *specialized* demands from the earth, especially for our food."

—WES JACKSON[1]

We humans, in an effort to meet our demands as a species, have altered the face of the earth. We have cut down and planted forests, dammed and dug rivers, blasted

---

1. Jackson, *Altars of Unhewn Stone,* 148.

mountains and built hillsides, and churned the soil to grow our food. Bridges, walls, wells, and of course cities wind their way over the surface of the planet. We have thoroughly shaped the earth as a child bulldozes sand on the playground.

For the most part, the earth has bent her back to support us. Despite droughts, floods, volcanic eruptions, and earthquakes, many of us are still here, able to sit peacefully in the garden and give thanks. The problem is that many people in industrialized society have forgotten to give thanks. We are so used to our houses, cars, grocery stores, and other human inventions, we easily forget the larger cycles that make these many gifts possible.

One place we can begin to remember the earth's sacrifices, witness the miracle of the earth, and give thanks daily, is in the garden. It is our responsibility as lovers of the earth to remember where we stand as one species on a planet. It is our responsibility to teach our children and our neighbors about the intricate and precious connection we share with the land.

Most of us know this interconnection in our cells but deny it in our habits of daily living. We talk about the "environment" as an *other*. Our cultured minds think of ourselves as not-nature, not-environment, not-earth. While in many ways we are distinct from the earth, we are also of the earth. Our bodies know this even as our minds deny its truth.

Even those of us who consider ourselves "environmentalists" live in houses with electricity run by coal power, drive a car, purchase clothes made from chemically treated fibers, eat food shipped from a thousand miles away, and wear mined gold on our fingers. We long to live in harmony with the earth, but many people cannot afford solar panels, organic hemp clothes, or hybrid cars. We feel too small as one person to change a sick system.

The garden, however, is one place where anyone can be a part of the solution. When you plant an organic seed in compost made from your own kitchen waste, water it from mindfully gathered rainwater, and eat it mere feet away from where it was harvested, you feel your connection with the sacred land. You live in integrity. You share a reciprocal and active relationship with the land. Organic gardening begins to heal the earth by reducing our reliance on fossil fuels, trapping carbon gasses in the soil, and reducing our use of water for lawn care.[2] Gardening can heal a community by improving neighborly communication, providing beauty, and even reducing crime.[3] It also begins to heal the panic we carry in our bones, a panic that comes from a pervasive, destructive relationship with the earth. Gardening is a perfect example of what Buddhists call right relationship.

Have you ever come clean with a friend, clearing up an untruth? While honesty can be painful at times, it heals the spirit. Your body relaxes. You literally breathe more easily. Gardening is telling the truth: I depend on the

---

2. Danaan, *Sacred Land*, 48–49.

3. Ibid., 106–107.

earth. We live in reciprocal relationship. I cannot deny that humans shape and mold the earth to meet our needs and desires, but I can be honest about that relationship and actively participate in it in a mindful and constructive way. In the garden, I can live in integrity on the earth.

When we begin to tell the truth about living on earth, we realize what a responsibility we have to the planet. We have lived like selfish toddlers, believing that the earth will always provide regardless of our actions. It is time for us to grow up and take responsibility for our actions. The planet cannot continue to support us if we do not tell the truth and change our habits. Those of us who know this truth feel this responsibility most keenly.

Matthew Fox writes in *A Spirituality Named Compassion,* "Most compassionate people I know work with the soil whenever they can. Gardening for them is much more than a hobby. It is a way of life and a way of wisdom. The soil teaches us something that is necessary for becoming compassionate."[4] Gardening is in itself a spiritual practice. It is a way to listen to the land, slow down, and pledge your compassion for the earth in a very real way. We have changed the face of the earth and have caused an awful lot of suffering in that process. But a spiritual path of listening to the earth—especially when that includes active relationship with the earth through the garden—can help respond to that suffering in a very real way. The garden can heal our suffering, the suffering of our neighbors, and

---

4. Fox, *A Spirituality Named Compassion,* 173.

the suffering of the earth. It creates a life of compassion and integrity.

If you don't consider yourself a gardener, you live in a small apartment, or you have little time to garden, I encourage you to bring the power of gardening into your life through potted veggies and herbs and friends' gardens. Our current food system is not sustainable. We must begin to be more directly involved in the raising of our own food. There are many ways to participate in the power of gardening, from starting a few pots of your favorite veggies to buying a share on a community-supported agriculture (CSA) farm to helping a friend weed her own garden in exchange for some of the harvest. You may find that one step leads to another as you learn more and let the magic of gardening cast its spell.

DEEP LISTENING TO THE GARDEN

The following meditation brings you into a deeper awareness of the miracle of the garden. Read it through once or twice, then go outside into any garden space to practice the meditation.

❧ FIND A COMFORTABLE spot outside in a vegetable or flower garden. This can be done any time of year, but will be most dramatic in spring or summer. Take time to ground and center. Follow your breath and open to your senses while letting your mind be calm. Smell the breeze, the soil, and the plants. Listen to the wind, the birds, and the squirrels. Gaze gently in front of you, simply witnessing what there is to see. If appropriate, you may want to pluck a few edible leaves or a vegetable and savor its unique flavor. Feel your butt or your knees on the ground. Run your palm lightly over the soil, mulch, or ground cover. You may want to get up and walk through the garden, observing, or simply let your gaze fall where it will, taking in the landscape. Let your mind be calm, noticing any thoughts that arise and releasing them like a butterfly into the breeze.

Find a comfortable position and take another deep breath, including your own body in your awareness. Follow your breath into your lungs, then out into the garden. The plants will use the carbon dioxide you have exhaled, manufacture oxygen, and release oxygen for you to inhale. Sit for a few moments breathing with the plants.

Send your awareness downward, into the soil beneath you. Feel the type of soil, the density of particles, strains of rock or water, and the billions of creatures that live in soil. Bacteria, fungi, nematodes, worms, and insects live in the kingdom of the earth. There may also be burrowing mammals, newts, or frogs nearby. Laced throughout this subterranean world are roots of the trees and plants. Let your awareness vacillate between an intellectual awareness of this kingdom of earth, and the sensations moving through your body as you attune with the ground beneath you.

Focus on a plant in front of you, and become aware of its roots reaching into the soil for water and nutrients. Feel the whole plant, from its hairy root tips up through the stem and into the edges of its leaves. Here is another breath, an exchange of gases, minerals, and water spiraling into the soil through the plant and into the sky.

If this is a vegetable, herb, or edible flower garden, the exchanges of nutrients and elements will become a part of whoever will eat the produce or drink the herbal teas. Here is a spiral network through time as well as space: the garden is connected to all around it, to all that nourished it in the past, and to all who will consume it in the future. When you eat food grown in your own garden, you become a part of your land and it of you. The minerals in the soil become the minerals in your cells. The energy of the sun used by a plant to grow its own food becomes your energy.

Which minerals exist in this soil depends on the geography and history of the land. Glaciers, stones, rivers, volcanoes, and the shift of tectonic plates deposit inorganic matter on the land, matter necessary to support life. Weather also shapes the land. The earth is always changing. At this point in time, we are able to live on the planet because of a long list of inorganic processes, from the formation of the solar system that deposited certain elements here, to the formation of the moon that keeps our planet on its axis, to the location of the continents that give us temperate land to inhabit. A garden cannot exist without adequate minerals, nor can it exist if the weather gets too extreme.

Sit for a few moments absorbing the miracle of these life cycles. Give thanks to the planet, the sky, rain, and the sun. Give thanks to the garden.

Ground and center, and stretch when you rise to anchor yourself in space and time.

Garden Intelligence

Gardening is in itself a spiritual practice, but you can deepen that practice and grow a more vibrant garden by working with plant spirits. The spirits of the garden include the energies of each plant, garden devas, fairies, and elementals, to name a few of the unseen beings and forces of the garden. These beings can be our partners in creating positive change and healing. When you learn to communicate with the unseen spirits of the land through your garden, you take your work as a gardener and earth healer to another level. You are no longer manipulating the land to meet your needs, but are actively working with the intelligence inherent in the land, plants, soil, and so on.

Intelligence means much more than a central nervous system, but includes knowing, intent, and intuition. A deep intelligence or wisdom about *how things work* pulses in the very fabric of the earth. We can see this intelligence in natural cycles: Grass transforms sunlight into energy; ruminants like cows have just the right stomach to digest grass fibers, transforming grass into cow energy; some of the excess not used by the cow is plopped back onto the soil as fertilizer, while the cow's hoofs loosen the soil, allowing air and water to penetrate the surface.

Beneath this and the billions of other reciprocal cycles on earth is another intelligence: the spirits of grass, soil, cow, wind, and rain. "[Intelligence] is an organizing flow from the soul to a physical focal point, and it flows through the form," writes Machaelle Small Wright.[5] Inside or beneath form is the flow of intention and purpose that is expressed through form, whether that form be a cow, a human, or a blade of grass. That organizing force is found in nature spirits such as devas, plant spirits, and fairies.

Which form of nature energy you interact with in the garden depends on your intention. A deva is the creative and architectural energy of a plant; the tomato deva is in charge of the creative and architectural expression of all tomatoes on earth. A plant spirit is more specific, the spirit of one tomato plant growing in your garden.[6] A fairy, gnome, or other individual energy is an ambassador from the energetic realm, a bridge between form and pure energy.[7] Therefore, if your intention is to ask a single sick plant what it needs, you would attune with the plant spirit. If you wish to ground the energy of carrots in your garden after planting carrot seeds, however, you would call on the

---

5. Wright, *Co-Creative Science*, 27.

6. Ibid., 33.

7. Ibid., 35.

carrot deva. A fairy or sprite might appear if it is the best form of communication for you. I have personally never intentionally worked with fairies or gnomes because I attune directly with the energy I wish to contact. The most opportune method of communicating with garden intelligence at any given time may be different.

Nature intelligences have been historically dismissed to the world of myth and fantasy, but in the next few generations, they will become more accepted as "real" as we expand our awareness of other states of being. In *The Secret Life of Nature*, journalist Peter Tompkins researched the phenomenon of fairies and other nature intelligences. He discovered some interesting evidence of the truth of fairies when looking into claims of fairies by clairvoyant members of the Theosophical Society. Advanced practitioners of certain yogic skills were able to see other levels of reality, including subatomic particles and nature spirits. These people were able to describe details of subatomic particles that quantum physicists now regard as fact. They were also able to describe a complex world of devas, angels, gnomes, and fairies. Tompkins suggests that if the yogic clairvoyants were able to see a quantum reality that we now know to be real, the world of fairies is likely to be just as real. He writes:

> Although I approach the subject as a reporter, relaying extraordinary information described by clairvoyants—data that sometimes does indeed defy credulity—in the end I find their evidence so compelling and so rational that even though not myself clairvoy-

ant, I now tend to subscribe to their conviction that
to resolve the evils and problems of this world we
must all learn to commune with the world of nature
spirits and the angelic hierarchies from which they
derive.[8]

Keep in mind that we do not all have to be clairvoyant
(able to see energy) to interact with intuitive levels. You
may hear fairies or feel them. In fact, Tompkins writes in
his subsequent paragraph, "I do not see the spirits, but I
sense them all around me, and I no longer feel alone."[9]
I think Tompkins was a kinesthetic psychic. Learning
to work with the devas is a matter of practice and being
open to your abilities and their presence.

Nature Spirit Attunement

In this meditation you will again attune with a plant, with
attention toward that plant's unique intelligence.

♣ CHOOSE A PLANT in your garden to chat with,
perhaps your favorite plant or a crop that is doing
especially well right now. You might even choose a
particularly abundant weed, which also contributes
its energy to the signature of your garden. Any plant
growing right now in your yard or garden will teach
you something about your unique plot of earth while
giving you an opportunity to open to the realm of

---

8. Tompkins, *The Secret Life of Nature*, xi.
9. Ibid.

the nature spirits. This can be done any time of year; you may also work with a houseplant, but I recommend going outside if possible.

Sit before this plant, ground and center, and ask the plant permission to attune with it. Sense the answer in your own style. Soften your boundaries and reach out to the plant, entering into its vibration. It will reach out to you in turn.

Introduce yourself to the plant and thank it for being in your garden. Even if you work with a weed, thank it for contributing its unique gift to this land, for even weeds provide gifts. Bindweed, for instance, helps to connect and bind disturbed earth. Dandelions exhale ethylene gas, which helps orchard fruit to ripen quickly. Each of the vegetables, herbs, and flowers in your garden beds contributes their own unique energies and magical qualities. What will grow in your climate, and what you choose to grow based on your own tastes, reflects and shapes the energy of your garden and your home.

As you attune with this plant, sense what it gives to the land. The way it vibrates, the taste it leaves on your psychic tongue, tells you something about its properties and gifts. Notice how this plant vibrates with the land, making one thread in the tapestry of this unique plot of land.

If you have any questions about your garden—such as where to put a fruit tree, how to contour the space to more effectively use water, or what nutrients the soil currently lacks—ask this plant. Its answer may be different than the answer you would get from another plant, or from asking the garden deva spirit of your garden, but the plant will offer useful suggestions based on its own perspective.

Ask the plant if it needs anything to better express its unique gifts. Be prepared to carry out these requests after your meditation.

Now, if you want to open to another level, ask to speak with the deva of this plant. You will see or feel a slightly different consciousness when you open to the plant's deva. Speak with the deva as you did the individual plant.

Thank the plant and its deva for working with you. Draw your energy back into yourself and ground and anchor to your core. Carry out any requests as you are able. Record your experience in your journal.

⚜

Your own garden or yard, or the plants growing on your balcony and in your neighborhood, can teach you a lot about the energy of the land and what it means to attune with the earth. Furthermore, by working with the nature spirits of your land, you not only hold the ability to grow a vibrant and healthy garden, you heal the relationship humans have with the earth. In an e-newsletter from the garden Perelandra, Machaelle Small Wright wrote about global warming:

The bottom line is we have no choice but to work with nature directly to get us and the world out of this situation. If we don't do this, we'll get into a scientific hit-and-miss situation with some solutions working and some "solutions" causing further problems. It'll take us forever to reverse this global warming thing. Nature can give us the straight line out. We must have the courage to act alone as individuals. . . . Remind yourself . . . that this problem keeps boiling down to each single individual. . . . It's the collective force of individuals [that] will turn things around.[10]

FURTHER EXPLORATION

Practice

Plant a garden in your own yard or in a community garden plot. Many community programs and university extension offices offer classes on gardening if it is new to you. Or, if you are not inclined to develop your green thumb, join a farm that offers community-supported agriculture (CSA). Your share in a CSA helps support local, often organic, food production. Keeping our food local and responsive to the ability of the earth to support us is crucial at this time of great earth shifts. For more on the value of local, organic food, see my book *Sacred Land: Intuitive Gardening for Personal, Political & Environmental Change* (Llewellyn, 2007), or Barbara Kingsolver's *Animal, Vegetable, Miracle* (HarperCollins Publishers, 2007).

---

10. Wright, "A Message from Machaelle," April 23, 2007.

Journaling

Spend time in your garden attuning with the energies of different plants and plant spirits. Ask to speak to different nature intelligences, like gnomes, fairies, and angels. Record your conversations in your journal by writing what you hear or drawing what you see or feel. Notice how your awareness evolves over time as you regularly practice garden attunement. Notice how your gardening choices are affected by these communications.

Art as Meditation

Pledge your garden to compassionate relationship with the land. Make or decorate an object that symbolizes this dedication, such as a statue, bird bath, bird or bat house, mosaic flower pot, or garden stepping stone. You can purchase kits for simple garden art from hobby shops and good toy stores. Every time you see your garden art, you will be reminded of your work as a garden activist working to heal the land.

seven

GREEN ALLIES OF TRANSFORMATION

When I was eight months pregnant, I decided to transfer my large and unruly collection of herbs from little plastic bags into glass jars. Surrounded with jars, labels, and baggies of herbs, I squatted in front of the shelf that would hold my dried plant friends. I poured each little bag into a jar, labeled it, and set in on the shelf in rough alphabetical order. A peace settled over me as I nested in our new house, the house our first baby would call home. I set aside the herbs I needed to make baby bum salve: calendula, beeswax, and lavender. I worked in silence, listening to the neighborhood, the house, and the herbs.

Herb dust filled the air. I had been working for about an hour when I started to feel nauseated. Morning sickness had not been a problem with this pregnancy, and I was surprised to feel any nausea so late in the third trimester. Then I realized it was the herbs. Though I had not consumed any of them, their dust and their energies were enough to overwhelm my sensitive body. I took a break until the dust settled and my nausea subsided. I asked my body if I could proceed and felt okay to do so. I sent a wave of respect to the herbs and continued working.

Then I came across an unlabeled baggy. It was a chopped-up root, but I could not identify it by sight. I sniffed at the bag and was rewarded with a sharp pang of nausea. The herb felt wrong to my body. My repulsion was so strong, I tossed the bag in the trash.

When I continued transferring and organizing my herb collection, I discovered at the bottom of the big box of baggies an errant label: black cohosh. Among other things, black cohosh is used to stimulate uterine contractions, and it has estrogen-like properties. My pregnant body wanted nothing to do with the little unlabeled bag of black cohosh, and I reacted strongly to just smelling the fairly odorless dried root.

HERBAL ENERGY

A special category of plant is the herb: intense little green beings that we use for their healing qualities. Herbs are plants humans use for medical treatment, nutritional value, food seasoning, or dyes. They are also often burned, smoked, or sprinkled in water or oil. Their focused powers of change and healing make them ideal allies, green beings who can help you on your spiritual path. Herbs

are special ambassadors to the magic and miracle of nature. They teach us about transformation and the energy-
shifting power of seemingly small things.

Herbs are taken internally, smoked, or worn in order
to change one's energy. You might drink an herbal tea for
improved health, smoke or burn some incense to calm
your mind, or wear a sachet to attract certain energies,
such as love or peace. Herbs can be special plant allies because they are worked with consciously and with intent.

When we use herbal medicines, flower essences or
homeopathic remedies, or eat certain foods to balance
your system and nourish your health, we work with plant
energies. The molecules in the plants exchange electrical charges with the molecules in our bodies, effecting
change at the subatomic level. We experience these energetic revolutions as improved digestion, better sleep,
or clarity of thought—but the initial changes occur in the
energetic matrix of the body, in the cells, molecules, and
subtle energy fields.

Some plant-based remedies are based entirely on subtle
energy exchanges, like flower essences and homeopathic
remedies. Flower essences, which are the energy of the
plant distilled into water via sunlight, alter our energy body
as soon as we contact them by placing the essence on our
tongue or drinking it in water. Homeopathic remedies
also work vibrationally, awakening the body's innate healing mechanisms by introducing trace amounts of a plant or
other substance into the body. The energy of the homeopathic substance stimulates the body's healing reaction.

For example, the belladonna plant can cause hallucinations, tachycardia, blurred vision, loss of balance, confusion, and other changes in the nervous system. When a patient experiences these symptoms, the homeopathic preparation of belladonna is used to awaken the body's healing mechanism, restoring balance and health in the system. In reaction to homeopathic belladonna, the body responds with improved strength in the heart and nervous system. The symptoms subside because of this improved strength rather than the suppression of symptoms, as in allopathic (conventional) medicine.

Herbs work because of their strong energetic fields, and the type of remedy depends on how this field affects us. Nettle works by nourishing while homeopathic belladonna works by stimulating balance. Both of these are energetic processes. Plants and humans are all a coalescence of energy. We are coherent vibrations of specific frequencies operating in a great field of interacting vibrations. Herbal healing comes about through energetic entrainment. You can, therefore, work with the energy of an herb by physically imbibing it or working with it on a purely energetic level.

If I don't have access to an herb or I need to fine-tune my connection with a plant, or if I am unsure of the safety of taking a plant internally for any reason, I attune to the plant energetically, working primarily on a psychic level. I use the psychic realm to access the physical. As Loren Cruden writes in *Medicine Grove*, "Form is an octave of consciousness."[1] We can interact with a plant's form to alter our consciousness, and we can work consciously on a psychic level to affect our form. We move in and out of the hierarchy of manifest reality—form to energy and energy to form.

THE PSYCHIC HERBAL REMEDY

Working with herbs psychically is similar to attuning with trees and the land. The difference is that you enter into relationship with a purpose and a request. You are not simply listening to the plant, but asking it for help with a specific issue. You seek change in your body through energetic interaction.

❧ CHOOSE AN HERB you work with frequently or are familiar with, like echinacea or a dandelion. You may find it helpful to have the plant in front of you, either fresh or dried; as your skill grows, you will be able to attune with a plant on the astral level without any physical contact. Ask the plant for permission to work with it psychically. You will probably be welcomed in, but if not, try another time. Trust your subconscious, the plant, and your spirit guardians to guide you away from interacting with a plant if the time is not right.

When you and the plant are both ready to work, ground and center. Let your energy open to the herb.

---

1 Cruden, *Medicine Grove*, 6.

Say aloud or in your mind, "I call on the energy of [plant name] and ask for your guidance in my journey of health." Take a moment to attune with the herb and be aware of its energy, its properties, and anything else you notice while sitting with the plant in psychic connection.

Present to the plant something in you that needs nourishment, such as an ailment or a difficult process you are experiencing. Ask the herb if it has anything to offer to help you with this concern, and how it can help. Sit for at least ten minutes listening, feeling, and being open to what arises. You may see images, feel sensations, or hear phrases.

When you feel finished or are saturated with all you can take in for one sitting, thank the herb for working with you. Pull your energy back into yourself. Take a few moments to ground and center again as needed. Record what you learned in your journal. You may feel it appropriate to offer a gift to the plant with which you worked, like a sprinkling of cornmeal or purified water on a patch of the herb growing in your garden.

Energy and Intention in Herbal Preparation

You will not always work with herbs in a purely energetic fashion; I've started there to show you that it is possible to work with green allies on a purely energetic level. Herbs are fun to work with because of their sensual physical nature, and by their very nature, herbs are all about drinking them, burning them, or soaking them in water, oil, or alcohol to utilize their physical properties. Herbal preparations like lotions, teas, and syrups have a highly desirable earthy sensuality about them. You can have the best of both worlds as well: When ingesting or physically working with an herb, you can enhance its potency and your alignment with its powers by connecting with the herb's spirit on an energetic level as well. Even when you work with an herb physically, you also do so on an energetic level, so including this energetic awareness deepens your relationship with your herbal creations.

Herbal preparations include:

- Tinctures: herbs preserved in alcohol, vinegar, or vegetable glycerin, which concentrates the herb's healing qualities
- Infusions and decoctions: essentially strong teas
- Syrups: a concentrated decoction sweetened and preserved with honey or glycerin
- Essential oils: plant oils extracted by steam or chemicals
- Infused oils: an herb soaked in oil
- Ointments, salves, and lotions: made by adding wax to an infused oil

These preparations can be purchased at herbal apothecaries and health stores, or they can be made at home (except for essential oils). To learn how to make your own herbal remedies, turn to the following books:

- *Healing Wise* by Susun Weed (Ash Tree, 1995)
- *Medicine Grove: A Shamanic Herbal* by Loren Cruden (Destiny Books, 1997)
- *The New Holistic Herbal* by David Hoffman (Barnes and Noble, 1995)
- *Rosemary Gladstar's Family Herbal* by Rosemary Gladstar (Storey Books, 2001)

While harvesting or processing an herb, as when grinding it with a mortar and pestle, let your energy reach out to the herb. Entrain with its energy. Feel its unique personality vibrating with your body and any disease or issues you face. Reach deeper into the spirit of the plant, seeing its divine light raising the vibration of your own body and spirit. Let herbal preparation become a meditation that infuses your remedy or beauty product with love and divine healing energy.

When you use a prepared herbal preparation, like a store-bought tincture, take a moment to give thanks to the herbs and the people who created this remedy. Thank the soil, water, and sun that gave the herb life. Attune with the energy of the plant and ask it to bless your healing process.

FAVORITE HERBS

There are many fine herbals from which you can learn about a plant's healing properties, chemical makeup, and applications. In our modern society, one can look up an ailment in a trusted herbal, get a list of the plants known to address this problem, and drive to a nearby health food store or shop online to get these herbs. Following a recipe, you put them together in the most appropriate remedy and consume them as suggested until your symptoms ease. When I get sick, this is one of my first responses. I find, though, that when I prepare the remedy with mindfulness and by attuning with each herb's energy, I feel a much deeper sense of wellness and connection. The herbs then become not just an application to a problem, but living beings with whom I am seeking change. The herbs journey with me on a path of conscious awareness and holistic healing.

I also find that working with a small number of herbs that I know well creates a sense of clarity for my healing. An attuned healer can actually use any one herb to address any imbalance by drawing on this subtle relationship. Shamans and witches have traditionally worked only with the plants they know intimately by growing, harvesting, and communicating directly with plants native to their own habitat. Through meditation, life experience, and affinity, they learn which herbs are their own plant allies. It is with these allies that they do most of their work.

If you have worked with herbs in the past, likely you have a few favorites—your herbal allies. These are the herbs you know best, use often, and trust most. You may have been acquainted with them since childhood. One of my own herbal allies, for instance, is stinging nettle. As a child in the Pacific Northwest, I knew them best as the plant to avoid in the woods. In the summer, they grew a tall as my father in small forests of stinging green leaves. In college I learned how to touch them safely by petting them in an outward stroke, as the little stinging, hook-like hairs poke toward the pointy end of the leaf. I learned they were edible and full of nutrition. After college I learned more about their healing properties, especially from reading Susun Weed's *Healing Wise*. Now I live in Colorado, where they only grow when cultivated near water. I purchase them dried from the store and drink them in teas. I feel a deep affinity with this magnificent plant and turn to it first whenever I need nourishment. When I visit my family in the spring, I pick the nettle buds and cook them in pasta or spanikopita.

To determine your herbal ally, consider who has been a powerful presence in your life. Journal about the following questions:

- What plants grew around you as a child?

- What grows wild in your backyard now?

- When you read the ingredients of an herbal tea, which herbs jump out at you?

- Which herbs do you grow in your garden, or in pots in the kitchen window?

- What plants have appeared in dreams?

- Have friends ever gifted you with a lot of one herb?
- Has one herb grown at several of your homes throughout your life?
- When someone says "herb," which plants come to mind?

You can also ask your herbal allies to reveal themselves to you in meditation, or become more aware of which herbs present themselves to you. I recently discovered a new herbal ally, usnea, when a series of coincidences brought it to my attention. Listen, and they will reveal themselves to you.

YOUR HERBAL ALLY

Here is a meditation to help you discover your herbal allies. This meditation can be used to discover herbal allies, temporary green helpers, or a plant totem, which would support you throughout your life.

♣ SIT IN A safe place where you will not be disturbed. Ground and center by following your breath and feeling your body on the earth.

When you feel ready, close your eyes. See your breath as a light entering into the top of your head with each inhalation and exiting out your sacrum or base chakra on the exhalation. Ask Mother Earth and Father Sky to guide you on your plant journey. Ask that they show you your place in the universe and your special plant allies.

See yourself standing at the edge of a forest. Vines and flowers grow beneath the trees. The breeze blows softly, and the air is comfortably warm. Bees buzz in the flowers growing at the forest edge, and birdsong fills the canopy far above you.

A pathway opens before you; you step into the soft green light of the woods. You ask the forest to guide you to the plants that wish to work with you at this time. As you walk, the forest around you begins to transform. You can see light emanating from the plants' leaves. You can feel the breath of the trees and the soil all around you. Take some time to walk in your spirit wood, sensing, seeing, and listening to the power of the plant world.

After you walk for some time, deeply attuned to the land, you come to an opening in the trees. Up ahead is an ancient stone temple, open on all sides to allow the breeze to play among its moss-covered columns. Its floor is dirt and moss. You approach the temple and ask if you might enter. From the land all around you comes an invitation to proceed. In the middle of the sacred earthen floor grows a plant. Ask now what this plant wishes to be called. Ask about its work on earth, and what it has to share with you. Inquire if it is your ally, a short-term friend, or a plant totem that will work with you throughout your life.[2]

---

2. Cruden, *Medicine Grove*, 39.

The plant offers you a small bit of itself to take with you. You pick off a leaf or flower, and place it in a pouch around your neck. In return, you offer it a strand of your hair. You thank the plant for working with you.

Return now up the path to the edge of the wood. Return through the forest to your body sitting in meditation, and open your eyes. Take several deep breaths and anchor to your core.

Feel the essence of your plant friend held in the spirit space around your heart, where you placed it in the pouch in your meditation. Record your journey in your journal, especially all your learned about your herbal ally.

⚜

Working with herbs in our modern society is often a more "natural" version of applying a drug's properties to something that slows us down. Approaching herbs on a holistic level, as a wise human who listens deeply to the signatures of each plant, brings a different approach to your life and the concept of health. You begin to see health as a dance, a continuum. It is a gift from the earth and from your own spirit. Health is about relationship with the universe, a relationship that can be gently aided and shaped by your work with certain plants. By living in holistic relationship with herbs on physical and energetic levels, you become more conscious that you are a part of the whole.

Further Exploration

Practice

Create an herb garden. Research the growing needs of your herbal allies and herbs with which you wish to work. Many herbs grow well in pots if you have little outdoor space, and pots can be a good introduction to gardening. Spend time in meditation with them regularly, getting to know deeper layers of each of the herbs in your garden.

Journaling

Explore in your journal how working with the energy and spirit of herbs brings you closer to Spirit. What have you learned in listening to herbs as teachers and guides? How does this affect your image of health and healing? What does it mean to have herbal allies as a part of your spiritual path?

Art as Meditation

Make a collage or drawing of your herbal ally. Press a fresh herb between two pieces of waxed paper and leave it in a book for a few weeks until dried. Glue the pressed herb onto thick cardstock or homemade paper. Frame the herb with descriptive words or phrases that came to you in meditation or that you have learned from books or classes on herbs. Decorate your paper altar with images you draw or cut out from magazines to illustrate the qualities of this plant. Hang your visual homage wherever you work with herbs.

eight

ENERGY OF THE ENTHEOGEN

I have never been particularly drawn to mind-altering substances, save the occasional glass of nice red wine. In high school I avoided the usual teenage experimentation (mostly out of fear), and it was not until after college that I tried marijuana. I don't really care for her numbing quality, nor the burn in my lungs. However, I am a plant person to my core, and I was curious about this plant that causes so much trouble and offers so much pleasure. Holding in my hand a marijuana bud a friend had given me, I went into a light trance state and connected with the energy of the plant.

My initial impression was of strength. A ropy stalk rises from sturdy roots, which have been shown to resist herbicides. The roots gave me an impression of adaptability, able to move almost anywhere. I don't know how well they transplant, but I did later learn that the plants are very adaptable to different soils and climates.[1] The maple-like leaves seem to glow with an intense green-white light that I haven't felt in many other plants. There is an Earth Mother quality to the female plant (the flower buds from the female plant are what we cultivate for narcotic effects). This plant is sturdy, short, has dirt under her nails, and doesn't shave her armpits. She has a great sense of humor, and finds the hubbub we humans have created today over the affects of her toxins pretty funny. She is happy to oblige.

I suspect that many people who feel drawn to regular marijuana use do so not only for its "mellowing" effects, but also to ally on some level with this strong Earth Mama. The plant slows a person down, enabling the user to participate in a different rhythm. Details become fascinating, often beautiful. Time flows more slowly as one becomes less attached to one's concerns. For many there is a desire to disassociate from the world, or to fit in with others who partake, but I believe that on some level this desire could also be a need to groove with the planet via a plant that dances to a deep earth beat.

I am not condoning or condemning the use of marijuana. I think most people who use pot as a vice should question what fears and anxieties they seek to numb with

---

1. Purdue University Center for New Crops & Plants Products. "*Cannabis Sativa L.*"

the plant. However, there may also be a deeper vibration sought in smoking pot, and I suggest that when the plant or any other psychotropic herb is approached mindfully, with respect and energetic awareness, that vibration can be found more readily. Herbs like marijuana, peyote, hallucinogenic mushrooms, and even catnip (a very mild hallucinogen for humans) can be powerful allies, but they can also cause a host of problems when they are used to escape the usual confines of human existence. Intention and approach can transform one's experience with these plants.

※

A woman I met in college rolled her own cigarettes and always sprinkled a little loose tobacco on the earth before smoking. She gave thanks to the planet for its gift, and she savored the cigarette while she smoked. I had never met a person who smoked cigarettes in a spiritually based ritual. When I first heard that Native Americans gave tobacco to the earth and their friends as a token of respect, I didn't understand. I hadn't connected the smelly, nasty habit of cigarettes with a plant, and certainly not a sacred plant. But the way my friend approached tobacco as a an earth-honoring ritual altered the way I viewed cigarettes. I saw how smoking could be a meditation, a way to attune with the powers of a plant, the earth, and our intentions for working with mind-altering plants.

Plants stimulate the body via their chemical properties, but also through a symphony of energies that include your mind, body, the plant's growing conditions, and so on. When two energy fields sit in proximity, like the ticking clocks used to illustrate entrainment, they share packets of energy, becoming more alike. Everything is energy expressed through form. Everything entrains with adjacent energy fields to some degree. A plant, whether it is lettuce, mugwort, or marijuana, carries in its cells subatomic packets of energy from the soil it was grown in, the mood of the grower, the rain or irrigation water that nourished it, the thoughts of she who harvested it and on up through its history to your intentions, feelings, and thoughts as you consume it. In *Medicine Grove: A Shamanic Herbal,* Loren Cruden writes of how she smoked a very large amount of marijuana without getting high, much to the chagrin of the owner of the pipe. Cruden thought it was a peace pipe of sacred tobacco and was simply honoring the pipe owner by smoking the herb in a ritual way. "Oriented to prayerful intent, and buffered by innocence, despite my past experience with marijuana, I had no realization that the herb I was smoking was marijuana, and received no drug effect from smoking it," she wrote.[2]

A negative frame of mind can affect one's experience with mind-altering substances as well. A friend of mine planned to eat psychotropic mushrooms with a group of his friends. He had already taken some of the mushrooms when his friends decided they weren't in the mood for 'shrooms. Just then his girlfriend called, breaking up

---

2. Cruden, *Medicine Grove*, 80–81.

with him, and he spiraled into a panic. Alone in his altered state, fueled by panic, my friend went a little berserk. He jumped through a plate glass window, had to be restrained by two burly cops, and woke up in the hospital with little memory of his experience. Mushrooms don't usually have this effect unless they are laced with another substance or the psychological state of the person taking them interacts with their energies in a way that sends him or her over the edge. My friend felt trapped when his friends abandoned him to trip alone, and his panic interacted with the mushrooms to turn him "into a maniac, and [he] was doing things consciously, but couldn't control [his] body."[3] He jumped through a window to escape this trapped feeling. He was unable to process the mushrooms on his own, whereas perhaps with his friends also tripping, or at least holding space for him, he might have felt safer and saner in the field of their shared experience. He could have been supported in his panic.

Because mind-altering plants affect the brain, nervous system, the subconscious, and the spirit, they must be approached with a great level of honesty. Cruden writes, "Plants can open doors for you, but if what you carry through those thresholds is the baggage of fear, confusion, egoic desires, insecurity, and illness of relationship, your journey will be circumscribed by those burdens."[4]

---

3. Anonymous, personal communication with the author, December 11, 2008.

4. Cruden, *Medicine Grove*, 85.

Your pipe is filled not just with your herb of choice, but also with your intentions, fears, and desires. Taking time before you light up to sift through those invisible ingredients will ensure a safer and more fulfilling experience. Time for introspection and honesty will help you separate ego fears from a pure longing for a heightened experience with the universe.

Psychotropic plants have been worked with since before recorded human history as a door into a greater understanding of the universe. Another name for a psychotropic plant is *entheogen*, which means "inducing a god within."[5] As humans have done for millennia, you may use entheogens to seek Spirit. This journey calls for integrity and experienced support.

When traditional indigenous peoples use psychotropic plants, they do so in a ritual fashion. Usually, psychotropic plant use among indigenous societies is not a recreational experience as much as a religious one. The user is attended by others who do not consume the plant but who have experience with the plant's unique trance state and have been trained on how to hold sacred space.

ENTHEOGEN ATTUNEMENT

An alternative to ingesting a mind-altering drug is to work with the plant psychically. Whether you lack spiritually grounded and experienced support or you wish to

---

5. Miller, "Botanical Divinities," *Science News*: 75–77.

avoid the alchemy of plant chemicals, neurotransmitters, and ego burdens, you may find psychic work a preferred alternative to ingesting an entheogen.

🌿 To WORK WITH a plant on a psychic level, gather a small piece of the plant before you. Work in a safe place where you will not be disturbed. Ground and center. Ask your guides and guardians for their support and protection, especially if this is a plant you have not worked with before, it is a particularly strong plant, or you have had challenges with the plant in the past.

Take several deep breaths and come fully into the awareness of your body. Feel the weight of your bottom on the floor or cushion, feel your heartbeat and breath, and notice any sensations present in your body. Notice emotions and mind chatter.

When you feel grounded, clear, and ready, reach your consciousness out to the plant. Ask if you may work with it on an energetic level. When you feel a resonance, allow your energy to take in the plant's energy. Notice how attuning with the plant affects the sensations and emotions in your body. Pay attention to your heart rate, breath, and equilibrium. Notice what feelings arise, and where on your body you carry these emotions.

Ask the plant if it has any particular gifts to share with you at this time. You may receive messages, images, insights, or new awareness. Give thanks for whatever the plant wishes to share with you.

When you feel complete, or when the plant pulls back from your energy, give thanks, ground and center, and come fully back into your own sensations. Let any residual energy from your experience return to the earth. If you still feel uncomfortably altered, ground and release energy by placing your forehead and hands on the earth.

DIVINE SPIRITS

When you do feel drawn to ingest a plant or mind-altering substance, doing so in a ritual fashion will help to align you with divine energies and spiritual work. Entering trance with others, working with people experienced with trance work and plant use, and working within intentional sacred space creates a safe container for work with entheogens. Even if you are only drinking wine, doing so with ritual-based mindfulness will bring greater depth to your experience.

You can also first transmute the substance with which you will work in order to align yourself and the plant or substance with Spirit. Transmutation, the act of changing one substance into another substance through energetic intention, cleanses toxins and brings a thing or person into greater resonance with the Divine. The following ritual can be used to transmute wine, marijuana, or another mind-altering substance for use in sacred ritual. Again, I am not encouraging the use of these substances, only offering you an alternative and more mindful way of working with them.

One Samhain (Halloween), I performed the following ritual with a circle of friends. These people, incidentally, did not have previous experience practicing transmutation. We had not done ritual together before. While this ritual was done on Halloween, it can be adapted for use at any time. It follows the form of magical ritual, so you may not feel drawn to use all of the aspects, such as casting a circle. The key part is the meditation we did with the wine.

✿

We gathered at the table where we would later share our Samhain feast. Candles illuminated the room. In front of each guest was a cup of wine, with cider and water available for those who did not want alcohol. I explained that once we cast the circle, we would need to stay in sacred space together until we opened circle at the end of the ritual. I gave my guests a very basic outline of the ritual and invited them to participate as they felt comfortable. We would first create sacred space, ground and center, and then transmute the wine for sacred work, a process I would guide them through. At that point, each person would have a chance to speak in honor of friends or ancestors who had crossed over, since this was a Samhain ritual. When finished, we would clear the space and open the circle.

To cast the circle, I grasped the hand of the person on my left, moving in a clockwise direction. I said, "Hand to hand, I cast this circle." We passed the chant around the circle until we all held hands. I said, "Hand to hand, the circle is cast. We are between the worlds. At this time we may un-grasp hands, but the sacred circle will remain un-broken."

I looked around the circle of friends and began the process of transmutation, where a substance is aligned with its highest divine nature. First I asked the group to taste their wine. Then I said, "Close your eyes, and take a deep breath into your belly. Become aware of the earth beneath you and the sky above. Breathe energy into your crown chakra at the top of your head and out your base chakra, into the earth. Bring to mind an image of the Creator. This might be a bright flame, a dancing light, a force of energy—something that feels like the Creator to you. This might even be a sound. Sit for a moment with the feeling, image, and sound of Spirit. We will come back to this image in a moment.

"See yourself sitting on the earth. Now with each breath, bring a bigger view into your awareness. Feel the whole earth beneath you. See it floating in space. Breathe with the planet for a few moments.

"See our solar system, with Earth a part of these cosmic cycles; see yourself sitting on the surface of Earth. Let your energy expand beyond the planet, into the solar system. Keep breathing. Expand your awareness into the universe, spreading out into infinity. Take a few moments to feel this." I paused. This process demands patience and focused attention.

"See your image of the Creator. See this Divine Presence in the universe, part of the universe. Now see it as a part of you. Meld your energy with the Creator. You are the Creator. You are the universe. Sit in this energy for a few minutes. Let yourself become saturated with divinity.

"Now open your eyes and place your hands around the glass of wine in front of you. Invite the wine in the glass to express its own highest divine energy. Let it express the same infinite power of the Creator as you, as the universe, as the Creator. You are not trying to change the wine, only inviting it into the vibration of its highest form. You and the wine are divine. You invite the wine and every cell in your own body to resonate as divine light.

"Come back into your body, which has been the center of the universe, but is now a body in the room with friends. Feel your bottom on the seat below you and your breath moving in and out of your lungs. I invite you to take a sip of your wine."

We discussed how our wine had changed. We agreed there was a deeper flavor, not necessarily better, but thicker, more vibrant. When I have done this exercise with water, I have found the water becomes like the clearest, most pure mountain spring. Working with wine or other substances is a little more complex than with water, for you are transmuting many things at once: the grapes, energies from the bottling process, the vintner's intentions and thoughts, and so on.

We continued our Samhain ritual, where we could speak about friends or ancestors who have crossed over. I wanted to transmute the wine and align with our highest power first to keep the space sacred and open. When we were finished with the ritual, we grasped hands, and said, "Hand to hand I open this circle," moving in a counter-clockwise direction. I finished with, "Hand to hand, the circle is open but never broken. Merry meet, merry part, and merry meet again." The room got noticeably cooler when we opened circle, a shift in energy I and several other people noticed.

Try the exercise of transmutation with any substance you will take into your body, including wine, food, marijuana, or water. See how it changes your experience. You will discover a deeper relationship with yourself, the universe, and the plant or other object with which you work. Over time, it may also shift whatever relationship you have with a mind-altering substance. Be sure to write about your ritual and the unfolding relationship in your journal. Writing about it will help you see hidden aspects of your sacred work and will record your journey with entheogens, as well as with Spirit. Working ritually with a plant honors the plant and your body rather than seeking a way to escape and get high. Plants and your body are both sacred, so the practice of transmutation and sacred ritual brings you into greater alignment with yourself and with Spirit.

To learn more about transmutation, see Sandra Ingerman's *Medicine for the Earth* (Three Rivers Press, 2001), or my own *Sacred Land: Intuitive Gardening for Personal, Political & Environmental Change* (Llewellyn, 2007).

FURTHER EXPLORATION

Practice

Next time you are faced with a mind-altering plant, try working with it differently. If you usually avoid and fear it, try just holding it and giving it honor. If you always partake, try touching the plant to your forehead in honor of the community and the shared experience. Or you might perform a group ritual, setting a different intent as a group and working to align your practice with Spirit and the plant's unique teaching.

Journaling

Mind-altering plants can be a loaded subject. Write in your journal about how you feel in your body while reading this chapter. What does it bring up for you? Fear? Resistance? Excitement? What does that tell you about your own relationship with entheogens?

Art as Meditation

If you regularly use a substance like cigarettes, wine, or marijuana, create a sacred space to store them. Find a tin or an empty cigar box and decorate it with images of Spirit, the planet, and other things sacred to you. If you have a wine rack or alcohol cabinet, write a prayer about your intent in aligning with your higher power. Write it on decorative paper and place it where you store alcohol. This is not to cover up any unhealthy habits with a pretext of spiritual expansiveness, but to remind you of the possibilities of sacred alignment when working with these substances.

nine

CREATURES
GREAT AND SMALL

When I was four years old, I declared that my middle name was Butterfly. My favorite shoes were navy blue clogs with light blue butterflies across the strap. I adored butterflies and felt an affinity with them. Years later, while in a guided meditation, I was shown my power animal, the butterfly. I have also had other animal guides appear to me in dreams or in real life though different phases of my life, like a wolf I dreamt of frequently during high school, and whale imagery that comes to me when doing any deep Reiki work or when I go through a period of transformation. Butterfly has always been what some Native people call my totem, and other animal guides have lent me their lessons and guidance through various life passages.

Shortly after college, I decided to pursue a career in healing. I applied for an administrative job at an acupuncture school while I took prerequisite biology classes and figured out what field to study. On the way to my second interview at the acupuncture school, I saw two butterflies dancing around each other while I waited at a stoplight. They flitted in circles together until the light changed, then flew away just before I drove into the school parking lot. I grinned, knowing the butterfly was a sign that this job would be exactly the right thing for me. I hoped the appearance of a pair of butterflies meant I also might meet my partner soon—but regardless, I knew transformation was in my future. This job was my emergence from the cocoon of childhood: It was my first real job after college, it lead me to a career in vibrational healing, and it taught me about confrontation, determination, and communication. It was also where I met my future husband.

At my wedding five years later, my husband and I were blessed with rabbit energy. It was an outdoor wedding on a former farm, and several gray rabbits hopped about behind the altar during the ceremony. A year later, we opened the messages our friends and family had written on little cards at the reception. One of our ministers had written, "By now the 'rabbit' and Venus [a gong we used during the ceremony] will have worked their magic. We would love to be part of the 'naming ceremony.'" I was, in fact, seven months pregnant. Perhaps the rabbits had nothing to do with my pregnancy, but certainly the fact that our rather psychic minister knew I would be pregnant within the year was notable. She named the rabbits as part of the energy of this process.

While we searched for the right name for our baby, I asked the land for a sign regarding her spirit animal. Later that day, as I sat in meditation in our backyard, a female kestrel perched on a nearby telephone pole. I had never before seen a kestrel, and I never saw one in my backyard again. One of the qualities of kestrel is that they hover for a while before diving for their prey. They are small and feisty hawks. My daughter was born late, in a quick and powerful labor. She is small for her age, but very strong and precocious. Definitely a kestrel.

※

A spiritual path of nature attunement includes fauna as well as flora. Working with animal guides and totems, animal dream work, and animal appearances offers another dimension to your spiritual evolution.

What animals appear to you regularly? With whom do you share your land? Animal allies offer another way to listen to Spirit. They offer us reminders of the cycles of life and the bigger picture of sharing a planet with many interconnected beings. Attuning to animal energies, though, requires an inner honesty with yourself. It asks for an advanced skill in allowing the earth to speak to you while going about its business on its own terms.

With the recent interest in Native American and other indigenous spiritualities, many people have become interested in the idea of power animals and animal guides. While this has brought a greater respect to indigenous cultures and to animals, there is a danger in projecting our ideas about spirituality onto the animals to whom we turn to guidance. We can forget that these guides are animals, living their own lives and worthy of their own space.

The animals around us, like the plants and stones and other people, are a part of the great network. They are mirrors of what we carry inside. Their messages and lessons are real, however, because we are all interconnected, and we are all mirrors of each other and the ever-unfolding present. Animal allies reflect messages from our own subconscious awareness. The animals, like us, are "a coalescence of energy connected to every other thing in the world," as journalist Lynne McTaggart writes in *The Field*.[1]

We are energy beings, non-human animals are energy beings, and the world around us is an awesome, complex network of energy interacting, reflecting, and dancing with itself. What you see in the messages of animals around you, in dreams and meditations, and in animal cards is pulled from the subtle and real movement of interacting energies. Each moment is a reflection of the holon of Life. A holon is something that is "a *whole* in one

---

1. McTaggart, *The Field*, xiii.

context, [and] simultaneously a *part* in another."[2] You are a whole person made up of parts, and you are also one part in a greater whole—communities, ecosystems, the planet, spirit groups, the universe; the list is endless.

Each moment contains the wholes of which we are parts, and if we pay attention, we can find reflections of our interconnections. Synchronicities, such as running into a friend you were just thinking of or animal appearances that offer the right symbolic message, are mirrors of our own inner world.

When we open to the messages and mirrors of the world presented to us through dreams, work with cards, animal presences, and other intuitive work, we open to the world of symbology and metaphor. These worlds are real. Our imagined journeys and imagined interpretations of animals, dreams, or plant communication are not less real for being imagined. Michael J. Haas writes in the magazine *Shaman's Drum*, "While we journey in NOR [non-ordinary reality], the spirit world connects with our imaginations and communicates in a language we can grasp—in symbols, pictures, metaphors, and stories."[3]

When you open to the world of symbolism, you do not have to be in an altered state to hear this language. You begin to see meaningful symbols all around you, especially in the animals like the butterflies I saw before my interview and the kestrel that showed me something about

---

2. Wilber, *Sex, Ecology, Spirituality*, 18.

3. Haas, "One Foot in Each World," *Shaman's Drum*: 50.

my unborn daughter. The world becomes a living dream. Then the interpretation is up to you.

Your Animal Ally

Each of us has what Native Americans call our own animal "medicine," meaning we ally with one animal who most reflects our unique energy. Mine is the butterfly. We also find allies as we go through certain phases or events of life. You can find your animal allies through meditation, dreams, and animal sightings.

Here is a meditation to connect with your own animal ally. You can read it through a few times and practice from memory, tape yourself reading it, or have a friend read it to you.

❧ FIND A SAFE space where you will not be disturbed. Close your eyes and take a few deep, cleansing breaths. Anchor to your core self by using your word, image, and movement (see pages 21–22). Feel your roots moving deep into the earth below you. Tune in to how your body feels in this moment. Try not to judge how you feel, just be aware.

When you are grounded and centered, visualize yourself at the edge of a forest. Feel your bare feet on the earth. A light breeze caresses your skin and lifts your hair. You feel comfortable and at peace.

There is a trail opening before you. You walk into the forest, listening to the birds and the wind. As you walk slowly along the dirt path, you reach out to gently touch the trunks and shrubs along your way.

You spot a body of water through the trees ahead. As you come into a clearing, you find yourself on the banks of a clear, blue lake. At the edge of the water you see a small box. You open the box to find a small item, such as a jewel, feather, or shell. You take off any clothes you are wearing, and walk into the water, carrying your gem. The water feels cool and refreshing, the perfect temperature. It is so clear, you see the bottom as it slopes gently away from you. You feel totally safe and at peace.

You dive into the water and swim with strong strokes into the deepest part of the lake. You see a hole at the bottom of the lake, which you swim through. As you come out through the hole, you find yourself in a field of wildflowers. Take a moment to feel the warm sunlight on your bare skin and to enjoy the beauty of the flowers all around you.

After a while, animals come to join you in the field. You feel perfectly safe with all of them, for they mean you no harm. You greet each of them, and may feel drawn to talk with some of them. Spend as much time as you like with the allies that visit.

One of the animals or insects will appear in each of the four directions. This is your spirit or power animal, your totem. Thank it for appearing to you, and for offering you guidance in this life. Offer it the gem or other item you brought with you from the lake's edge as a gift. Spend as much time as you like asking your power animal any questions, exploring the field with your guide, or just sitting in harmony with him or her.

When you feel ready, embrace your animal ally and thank all who have come. Dive up into the air, coming out into the lake. Swim to the surface and return to the shore. Gather your clothes and return back along the forest path to where you began.

Open your eyes and take a few moments to anchor and ground. Drink a cup of tea or eat some food to help you return fully to your body. Record your experience in your journal.

ANIMAL MESSAGES

Each of us has an animal guide and animal spirits that support us through our spiritual journey. In addition to these guardians, animals can appear to us as a part of the holon of the universe to reflect lessons and messages from Spirit. Learning to listen to these messages is an important part of developing your intuition. It can be helpful to have a few guides to animal symbols on hand as you learn the meanings of key animals. My favorite guides for interpreting this voice include:

- Philip and Stephanie Carr-Gomm's *The Druid Animal Oracle: Working with the Sacred Animals of the Druid Tradition* (Simon and Schuster, 1994)

- Jamie Sams and David Carson's *Medicine Cards: The Discovery of Power Through the Ways of Animals* (Bear & Company, 1988)

- Ted Andrews' *Animal-Speak: The Spiritual & Magical Powers of Creatures Great & Small* (Llewellyn, 1996)

- Sayahda's website, "Cycle of Power, Animal Totems," http://www.sayahda.com/cycle.htm

Guides to animal symbology draw on cultural archetypes and the collective unconscious. The symbols and meanings given also often come from either a specific culture (such as the Druids or Native Americans), from the author's own spiritual journeys with animals, or from a combination of both. You do not need an outside source like these guides, however. Use your greatest magical tool, your body, to attune with the holon of the moment. Connecting with the moment, the animal ally, and your surroundings through your body and psychic awareness will often lend even greater understanding than a guide. Using the tools of meditation, listening, and attunement, you can journey with the animals yourself.

By using the word *journey*, which is a shamanic term referring to advanced trance work, I do not mean to imply that you will be doing advanced shamanic work. Shamanic training is rigorous, specific, and not for everyone. I am not a shaman, and I am not trying to teach anyone else how to be a shaman. I use the word *journey* because we are all on a complex path together. We journey along the spider's web of life, learning from each other and deepening into ourselves.

If an animal appears in your life in a significant way, or in a dream or animal card (as in the two decks listed above), before you use another's tools to interpret the animal's meaning, take a moment to tune into your own body. Reach out to the animal with your attention. Notice any changes in your own body, including posture, breathing, tension, or pain. Notice if any images, emotions, or memories arise for you as you focus on the energy of this ally. Close your eyes and ground and center. Ask the animal what messages it has for you. Ask yourself what in you has attracted this particular animal today. Spend some time listening and feeling. Open your eyes, come back to your center, and give thanks to the animal for working with you today.

LISTENING TO AN ANIMAL

For a more detailed exploration of messages offered you by animals from dreams, cards, or in waking life, try the following meditation.

🌿 HAVE BEFORE YOU a picture of the animal that has appeared to you. Ground and center. Take a few deep breaths and settle into your body. In your mind, call out to the spirit of the animal you wish to talk with. Ask it for guidance and clarity. Thank the animal for appearing to you.

Hold an image in your mind of the animal as it came to you, whether in a dream or in nature. Sit for a few minutes focusing on this animal. Let associations, memories, images, and words arise in your mind. You may want to record these in your journal as they appear to you, or just remember them to write down later.

Ask the animal spirit what its message is for you today. Sit for a few moments to allow any words or images to appear in your mind like a fish rising to the surface of a pond.

If you wish to explore more deeply, imagine yourself becoming the animal. Feel how it is to move as this animal, to see the world from his perspective. You may even want to get up from your seated spot and move like the animal. Make noises like him. Look around you, and see the world through his eyes. What do you notice? How does your perspective change?

Come back to your spot, back to your body. Say aloud that you release the spirit of the animal. Shake him off your body, and feel yourself sitting in your human flesh.

Ground and center. Thank the animal for working with you, and offer a gift of blessing and prayer to this animal everywhere. Open your circle, go drink a cup of tea, and record your thoughts in your journal.

FURTHER EXPLORATION

Practice

Give thanks to your animal guide or power animal with whom you connected in this chapter's meditations by performing an act of conservation. Find an organization online that helps to protect your animal, and get involved. Try the World Wildlife Fund, http://www.worldwildlife .org, or the National Wildlife Federation, http://www .nwf.org. Learn about what this animal needs to have a safe and healthy habitat. Get involved with habitat care, either directly if the animal lives near you, or through an environmental organization. If appropriate, build a habitat for your animal near you. For instance, you might plant a butterfly garden or mount a bat house in your yard. If your ally is a domestic animal, volunteer with a local shelter or rescue organization. By working with your animal in the manifest world, you learn more about your ally while giving back to the network of compassion.

Journaling

What animals have appeared as themes in your life? Think back to powerful or difficult times, and consider what animals were a part of those transitions or events. In meditation or by using the guides listed above, research the meaning of these animals. They may offer new shades of meaning for you regarding these events. Record your discoveries in your journal.

Art as Meditation

Using cardboard, paint, sequins, feathers, fabric, markers, and anything else you like, make a Power Animal mask. Using illustrations from books, make a mask that represents the animal that appeared to you in this chapter's meditation. Hang it over your altar or in a place of honor in your house. You may even want to wear it, taking on the qualities of that being. How does it feel to become your power animal? Be sure to return to human form when you are done.

For more on making masks, see Lynn Andrews' *The Mask of Power: Discovering Your Sacred Self* (HarperSanFrancisco, 1992); *Maskmaking* by Carole Sivin (Sterling, 1986); and *Faces of Your Soul: Rituals in Art, Maskmaking, and Guided Imagery with Ancestors, Spirit Guides, and Totem Animals* by Kaleo and Elise Dirlam Ching (North Atlantic Books, 2006).

ten

EARTH
ALLY

On June 10, 1999, a ruptured fuel pipeline dumped almost three hundred thousand gallons of gasoline into Whatcom Creek in Bellingham, Washington. Ten-year-olds Stephen Tsiorvas and Wade King were playing at the banks of the creek with a lighter, and their little flame ignited the fumes from the spill.[1] The massive fireball burned off all of their skin, boiled the creek, and turned tens of acres of trees to tinder. The two boys later died of their injuries; eighteen-year old Liam Wood also died when he passed out from the fumes and fell into the water. He had been spending his summer afternoon

---

1. Nelson, Brunner, and Miletich, "Lighter Ignited Fire," *The Seattle Times,* June 17, 1999.

fishing at the banks of the creek. The blast killed thirty thousand salmon and trout in a river that had slowly been recovering from decades of logging and paper mills.[2]

When I read about the tragedy on the front page of the *Seattle Times*, my heart broke. I stood outside a grocery store, staring at the front page of the newspaper, and cried. It was on this creek, upstream from the explosion site, that I once taught sixth grade children about riparian zones, caddis fly larva, and trout habitat. I had spent time at the Whatcom Creek fishery with salmon fry. I had held in the palm of my hand a tiny brown frog that lived in a rotted log spanning the clear, swift water of the creek.

Reading about the explosion, I sobbed. What are children to think about the world when they learn to love a place and then this happens? I had worked so hard to teach my students about the holiness of the river, the trees, the land. What lesson does it give, though, when an ecosystem is destroyed by the violence of a clear cut, or when a neglected pipeline destroys the very ecosystem I am telling them to protect?

The loss of the fish, trees, soil microbes, insect larva—this grief hit me as hard as the death of the boys. Not only did I work as an environmental educator on this now-incinerated river, but as one who can energetically feel the land, I felt burned myself, in love with a doomed earth. I felt shaky, ill, and deeply sad.

2. Conklin, "It's a Time for Healing in Dead Zone," *Seattle Post-Intelligencer*, July 3, 1999.

I ache for a world where environmental disasters like this one would be impossible. Out of respect for the land and an awareness of our interconnection with all of life—including salmon, freshwater creeks, mountains, and sequoias—we would rely only on clean energy like solar power. There would be no fuel line to leak and explode. The salmon runs in Whatcom Creek would be healthy every year; we would know what was needed for their safety from listening to the river, salmon, land, and ocean, and we would carry out those requirements without question. Boys playing along the banks of every river in the world would grow up knowing how this river gives them life through clean drinking water, fish for dinner, and a clean and healthy home. They would know, too, how integral the river is to the land itself, and know how to live in harmony with this natural balance. They would be able to play safely.

In light of the Whatcom Creek explosion and many other daily ecological disasters, such a utopian world seems impossible. I believe, though, that were we in tune with our ability to hear the land, this dream world would not be impossible, but actually inevitable. We would know how to marry our technological knowledge with evolved spiritual awareness, because we would be developing these areas of information simultaneously in an integrated fashion. We would not only intellectually understand that we depend on the earth for our survival, but we would know it in our hearts and bodies and we'd have that deeply felt knowledge integrated with our logical thinking.

Your own work as a nature intuitive holds a key spot in this evolution. You are an Earth Ally, a crucial player in the game of planetary rebirth. You walk the earth during a powerful time, as humanity teeters between two futures: spiritual awakening and annihilation of our species.

Every generation has faced life-changing chapters, from the fall of Rome to the Renaissance to world wars and the Cuban Missile Crisis. But the era in which we now live is unique in its cataclysmic potential, for we are not just looking at a change in power or the death of a city or even a culture. We face extreme alteration of the planet's climate and the potential for sweeping extinctions not known since the dinosaurs vanished. Such changes are not, however, because of external, natural forces, but because of the greed, ignorance, and stubbornness of one species.

However, we may possess the power to save ourselves. We are, for the first time in human history, connected as an entire planet via the Internet and satellite television, indications of the evolved noosphere, the sphere of human thought. Through this interconnected mind, we can share the advanced technologies we have developed for clean energy, wise food production and distribution, and water purification. We can access brilliant minds and highly evolved spirits with the click of a mouse. We can learn from each other's triumphs and blunders on a worldwide scale. These connections, though, can only save us from ourselves if they are utilized in an integrated fashion, drawing on heart, spirit, and justice before greed, arrogance, and selfishness. Ken Wilber writes:

> Our massively increased means have led, for the first time in history, to an equally massive dissociation of the noosphere and the biosphere, and the *cure* is not to reactivate the tribal form of ecological ignorance (take away our means), nor to continue the modern form of that ignorance (the free market will save us), but rather to evolve and develop into an integrative mode of awareness that will—also for the first time in history—*integrate* the biosphere and the noosphere in a higher and deeper union. . . .[3]

And therein lies the entire point of this book: By developing and tuning in to your ability to understand the language of the earth, you are helping to integrate human wisdom and knowledge with the planet's biosphere. You are creating greater unity and healing on earth.

It is time to integrate the different levels of understanding into our daily practices, from growing our own food to listening to animal guides, fairies, and trees. This integration will be our salvation.

Salvation is a funny word, because it is so strongly affiliated with Christian doctrine. We use it to refer to the soul as an entity distinct from the body. Some fundamen-

---

3. Wilber, *Sex, Ecology, Spirituality*, 168.

talist Christians and Muslims believe that salvation will come only with the destruction of the physical world. As Jim Marion asserts that our salvation will come through the body,[4] I assert that our salvation is about the physical world as well. Both our continuing existence as a species and our evolution as spiritual beings depend on learning to live respectfully and harmoniously on the planet.

I believe we are born on earth to grow as spiritual beings and to learn to love. What better place to learn about unconditional love than a planet that provides us with everything we need to survive? Not just the planet, but the universe makes it possible for us to live. The moon keeps the earth on her axis, so that oceans and weather patterns remain fairly consistent. The outer planets' gravitational forces deflect meteors from striking the earth, which made it possible billions of years ago for the surface of the earth to cool sufficiently to support life. The size of our sun, the ozone layer, and the perfect balance of nitrogen and oxygen in the atmosphere all allow for human life. Much more oxygen, and the planet would ignite; much less, and we would suffocate. Our relatively temperate climate is also due to the location of the continents and mountain ranges, which affect air and water flow.

I am able to write these words, and you to read them, because of gravity, oxygen, the moon, the sun, soil, lightning, ocean currents, Saturn, the nature of water, and carbon. Taken together, these and other forces create a

---

4. See page 18.

miraculous, fathomless gift: life as we know it. I sincerely hope human life, the plants and animals we share our home with, and the planet itself will continue to exist for a long time. All things must come to an end, but preferably this will only happen when cycles have completed themselves naturally. I believe we have a lot of work to do as spiritual and physical beings, and I hope we can integrate our knowledge and open our levels of awareness sufficiently to play out the cycles of spiritual evolution we came here to enact. Our blessed planet is a companion in this process.

ATTUNEMENT WITH THE EARTH

Let us take a moment to attune with the earth in order to get a greater idea of her energy and our place on the planet.

    ❧ GROUND. CENTER. BREATHE. What is the earth? She is the planet that supports you. She is the celestial body that sufficiently warps space and time so as to pull your body to her like a mother holds her child. She is home to millions of species: soil microorganisms, anaerobic sea worms, cedar trees, lions, lichens crusted on rocks, albatross, scorpions, periwinkles, fruit bats, peonies, bush babies, kingfishers, gorillas, and humans. She is volcanoes, the jet stream, ocean currents, and tectonic plates.

    Sit with her. Sit on her. Sit within her. Breathe.

Now go deeper. Expand your energy, your body of awareness, so that it becomes one with the air around you and the soil beneath you. Breathe. Stay with the sensations, riding them like a pelican on the sea. Notice—do not judge, do not name or resist, just notice. Expand your sensing farther, into the neighborhood, the forest, the city, the land. Feel the mountains; reach to the sea. Take your time.

Feel your roots deep in the earth. The topsoil, stones, bedrock, water veins, molten core. Keep breathing. Keep expanding, taking in as much as you can in little bites. Slowly, become one with the earth. Feel her breath. Feel weather shifting, birds tilting through the wind-swept skies, whales dipping through the weight of frigid waters.

If you get dizzy or overstimulated, notice your own body. Notice your breath. Then as you feel ready, return to feeling into the earth.

Sit with her for as long as you like.

Bring your energy back into your own body. Go slowly. Breathe deeply. Anchor to your core self. Feel your heart beat, the tingle of your blood, the nerves inside your skin, and the weight of your bones resisting against gravity.

Rise and stretch. Open your circle. Write about your dream of the earth in your journal.

THE LIVING PLANET

Thousands of volunteers, the city of Bellingham, and local environmental organizations have toiled at the banks of Whatcom Creek to restore the devastated ecosystem. Slowly, insects and fish return. Tiny trees push roots into the soil. Money from Olympic Pipeline Company was used to rebuild the park, and nearby land purchased by the company from a developer has been designated a nature reserve. The families who lost their boys will never be the same. The creek will take decades to recover. But with care, attention, and dedication, healing can come to the land.

We are partners with the earth, learning to love, heal, and care for all life by incarnating on this planet. We can heal. We can live in harmony with each other. I think we as a species have to set that as our primary goal before we can end the destruction. Each of us Earth Allies has a role to play in our awakening as a species.

EARTH ALLY'S QUEST

You can become more clear about your destiny and life path by listening to the natural world with your heart, mind, and body. Tune in to the earth to see your own role in the deep unity of the noosphere and the biosphere. Return to the following meditation as often as you need clarity about your own life purpose as an Earth Ally.

♣ IN PREPARATION, CREATE a sacred altar in an outdoor spot in your yard or another sacred outdoor spot. The altar can be simple, a cloth spread on the ground on which you set a few sacred items. Include a stone or a dish of salt, some incense, an image of your power animal, a dish of water, and a votive candle in a tip-proof, wind-proof jar. If necessary, you can practice this meditation inside, but first clean your space of all clutter and smudge with incense to clear energetically.

After you have prepared your altar, take a cleansing bath. Sprinkle a little salt and your favorite oil into the water, giving thanks to the water, the sun, and the earth for the gift of your bath. If you are in wilderness, you might take a dip in a lake or river. Soak for however long you like, charging the water and your body with healing energy. Feel into the consciousness of the water. Feel your divine power and the divinity of the water. Let the bath dissolve and transmute all thoughts of fear or self-doubt. When you drain the tub, bless the water as it returns to the local water treatment system. It will bless all it encounters. Give thanks.

Dress simply and comfortably. Go to your sacred spot. Light the candle and incense (take care to secure both away from any flammable material). Sit in a comfortable position before your altar, and take time to ground and center. Follow your breath. Feel the wind on your skin, the solid earth beneath you, the warmth of the sunlight. Take in the smells and sounds around you. Breathe, and feel the earth breathe with

you. Become part of the earth. If you are indoors, include your home's wood and metal in your awareness,
then stretch beyond the building to attune with the
local environment.

Ask the earth, an animal guide, or a plant ally to
help you learn about your path on earth. Be still for
a moment, then ask that it be revealed to you with
whom you will work at this time. A plant, animal, or
spirit guide will appear to you in your mind, as a felt
sense, or possibly quite solidly before you.

Reach your energy out to the guide, and ask,
"What is my part as an earth steward? What am I
here to do?"

Then be still and open. Listen, feel, and allow im -
ages to flow through your mind. Phrases, memories,
or associations may drift to the surface of your consciousness. When you feel your mind wander, gently
come back to stillness and re-attune with your guide.
If you notice tension or fear in your body, let it flow
into the earth to be transformed. Take as long as
you need to listen. What does your animal, plant, or
spirit guide reveal to you at this time? Each time you
enter into this meditation, you will uncover another
snippet, a gift to guide you along your way. We are
not usually given our full life purpose at once, but a
little morsel of clarity help us along the path.

When the messages come less frequently, or you
are informed that this is enough for now, thank the
guide and pull your energy back into your body.

Breathe, ground, and anchor to your core. Go have a cup of tea, and record what you discovered in your journal.

Return to this meditation and your connection with the earth any time you seek guidance. When you feel lost, confused, depressed, or angry, turn to the earth. I always find a sense of peace and receive a vision of a larger perspective when I tap into the voice of the earth. I turn to the land for companionship and guidance whether I struggle with large issues like earth shifts, or with more personal things like my life path. All is part of the greater holon, and all issues can be seen from multiple perspectives. The land is a great place to find that perspective, for it responds without judgment or personal projection.

A single tree in the Amazon rainforest can be home to hundreds of species of insects, several orchids and bromeliads, birds, butterflies, and fungi. I think of our life purpose as a rainforest tree. It is complex, revealing bits at a time to the sun. As the tree grows, the other life forms evolve with it; some plants die and new ant colonies move in. Vines wrap themselves around new sections of trunk, and orchids bloom into the changing light. Your life purpose evolves over time, and you need not understand the whole of the great tree. Focus on one butterfly, one orchid at a time. Let it metamorphose or bloom, and see what is revealed.

Harder still than sensing your purpose in the grand scheme of planetary unfolding is knowing how to apply it to your life. What does it mean to be an Earth Ally? To discover and develop your ability to communicate with cedars and orchids, mountains and tadpoles?

The greatest tool for knowing how to integrate your awakening wisdom into daily life is trust. In the 1991 film *What About Bob?*, the title character has to learn to move through his fears by taking "baby steps." The phrase becomes a mantra for him. I feel for Bob. We so want to know the big plan. We want to know how it all fits together and what we need to do to move things along in the right direction. Trusting in the universe, our spirit, and the land as the great rainforest tree of life pushes toward the sunlight means taking baby steps as the path appears before us.

My own path has been as winding as a liana vine climbing up its host trunk. I studied art, psychology, and environmental education in college. Then I studied massage and energy healing. I have attended three graduate schools in three different subjects. Not knowing how this all fits together (besides tickling my fickle Aquarian nature) unnerves me at times. When I feel scattered and lost, though, I use my connection with the wisdom of the earth to settle and ground into the moment. Like the day I drove to meet a favorite author, attuning with trees along the way, I tap into the roots in the soil and the churn of the seasons to know I am in the right place for me at this moment. The land soothes as well as guides. I am beginning to see how my path holds together. I am beginning to trust my boots, as they say in hiking. Trust the path, trust your grip on the rock, keep going, and the vista will be revealed.

Sometimes the Earth will send signs to those of us who open to her voice, messages about our purpose and path. These signs keep us on track and offer encouragement. One of my favorite visitors came a week before I was offered my first book deal. I sat at the computer in the living room one night, fitting in some work after the baby was in bed. My husband was out in the garage, in his makeshift music studio. I heard a chittering noise outside. I knew instantly it was a bat. I slowly opened the front door, fearing it might fly in, and found my cat staring down at a tiny, grounded bat. I scooped up the cat and locked him and his sister in the massage room, and ran to get my husband and a box. We went out to the little bat, his wings spread out on the sidewalk. Bats cannot take off from the ground like a bird, and this one was hurt. I knew he would die if we left him. I also knew one is never supposed to pick up a hurt bat; people are only bitten by them when they try to pick them up from the ground. I could not leave him to the neighborhood cats, though. Our hearts pounding, we carefully wrapped him in a towel and put him in the box. He scowled and scolded us gentle giants. His courage brought tears to my eyes. Conferring, we decided to put the box in a nearby tree to at least get the little warrior off the ground. He climbed up the bark and we never saw him again. I can only hope his little wing healed and he was able to fly.

Bats teach us about shamanic death, flying into the dark sky, like a mother's womb, to be reborn each night. At the very least, I felt blessed to be so close to one of my favorite, deeply sacred creatures. I hoped, too, that his visit might foreshadow my own rebirth as an author. A few days later, my editor called to offer me a book contract. I gave thanks to the bat for giving me the heads up and blessing my journey in its little way.

Open yourself up to the signs around you, whether they come from meditating with a tree or the visitation of an animal guide. Attune with the earth, and share your wisdom with others as you feel safe doing so. It is time to unify the earth with our own human knowledge, and vice versa. It is time to heal the rift between our earth bodies and our scientific minds. It is time for wholeness.

Whatcom Creek is the burn victim who lived. It recovers slowly, a testament to the lives of three boys. Near the site of the explosion rises a seventeen-foot totem pole carved by Lummi craftsmen in honor of the boys who lost their lives. When I reach out to the creek from Colorado, it shows me how the explosion was a gift, a call to us humans to wake up. The salmon need us as much as we need them. The sandy river bottom relies on us to protect and cleanse her—and we on her to carry our spirits to the sea. The stonefly creeping under slick loaf-sized granite rocks will feed the birds, who fill the skies with music. The interwoven dance of compassion and support that holds together the fabric of the earth relies on our learning to listen, love, and respond. It is time to look deeply at the thread we each hold in our own two hands. Our salvation lies in our bodies, in the earth, and in our hearts.

Many blessings, reader. Walk softly upon the earth, with a life of love and integrity. Open to the magic of the land, and share your song with others. Namasté, Amen, and Blessed Be!

FURTHER EXPLORATION

Practice

For a deeper exploration of your path, you may want to go on a vision quest. There are still native teachers who offer quests; ask around to find the right teacher for you. Look for people trained in ecopsychology, wilderness therapy, or genuine indigenous shamanism. Listen to your instinct to find the right fit. Or you may want to research organizations that offer vision retreats, like the Animas Valley Institute in Durango, Colorado, http://www.animas. org; Circles of Air, Circles of Stone in Putney, Vermont, http://www.questforvision.com; and Wilderness Rites in Ashland, Oregon, http://www.wildernessrites.com.

Journaling

Write in your journal about actions you can take to carry out the wisdom you found in meditation. What little things can bring you into alignment with your path, like volunteering for a non-profit close to your heart? Are there long-term plans you can make that align with your vision, like taking classes or finding a new job? What steps do you need to take to move toward these goals? Write also about your fears and resistance in seeking these changes. Fears hold a lot of wisdom, and we can only learn their lessons and move beyond resistance by looking our fears in the eye.

Art as Meditation

Make a prayer necklace. Get light-colored, air-hardening clay or another medium of your choice from a local hobby shop. State aloud your intentions for you life and the earth; as you make your beads, hold these intentions in your heart. Roll the clay into little balls, about ¼- to ½-inch in diameter. Poke a toothpick or needle through the middle, wiggling it a little to make the hole large enough to accommodate a string. Let your beads dry for a few days, then paint them with colors that remind you of your path. String them on fishing line or thin leather cord. When you pray or meditate, hold the string of beads in your hands. You can finger a bead at a time like a rosary, wear it on your wrist like a Buddhist mala, or simply hold it to align you with your life work.

SUGGESTED
JOURNAL TOPICS

$\mathcal{H}$ere are suggested journal topics from the text. If you feel stuck, try choosing one of these topics to write or draw about.

- Looking Deeply—Find a tree or bush outside or sit before a potted plant. First look at the plant without labeling or analyzing. Try to simply look, letting your mind be still.

- Find another natural object to observe, and on a fresh page, list every word that comes to mind as you look closely at this object.

- Free write all of your observations of your surroundings. Include body sensations and information from all of your senses.

- Write about your journey to work.

- What do you notice while playing in the backyard with your children?

- What do you notice while watching the sunset?

- Where is the moon in her monthly passage? What is the weather like and how does that feel in your body?

- What is growing in your garden or neighborhood right now?

- Journal about the sensations in your body. Include memories and emotions.

- Write about the body mapping exercise found on page 28.

- How do you pick up psychic information? In what form does it come to you?

- Journal about your listening experience with a plant. Were there some trees or plants that felt more comfortable to you? Did some ask you not to attune with them? Could you sense why?

- Write about how living with plants, stones, and rivers as individuals might affect you and how you might live your life differently.

- What is your experience of attuning to your home land and neighborhood?

- What kind of land do you affiliate with or feel drawn to?

- Write about attuning to waterways near your home.

- How does it feel to put down roots by planting a tree or garden?

- Write the story of home. What does home mean to you? Where do you feel most at home?

- Write about attuning to your house and your house blessing.

- Write a letter to your house. Tell it all your dreams for remodeling, for your life, and for its care.

- Journal about your garden meditation and attunement; also about attuning with garden devas or fairies.

- What do you experience when attuning to herbs?

- Your herbal ally: answer the questions on pages 114–115 about herbs; record your herbal ally meditation.

- Explore in your journal how working with the energy and spirit of herbs brings you closer to Spirit. What have you learned in listening to herbs as teachers and guides? How does this shift your image of health and healing? What does it mean to have herbal allies as a part of your spiritual path?

- Journal about transmutation.

- Mind-altering plants can be a loaded subject. What does the topic of entheogens bring up for you?

- Record your experience of the animal ally meditation.

- What animals have appeared as themes in your life? Think back to powerful or difficult times, and consider what animals were a part of those transitions or events. In meditation or by using the guides listed on pages 140–141, research the meaning of these animals. They may offer new shades of meaning for you regarding these events. Record your discoveries in your journal.

· Record your experience of the "Attunement with the Earth" meditation found on page 153.

· Journal about your Earth Ally's Quest. Write about actions you can take to carry out the wisdom you found in meditation. What little things can bring you into alignment with your path? Are there long-term plans you can make that align with your vision? What steps do you need to take to move toward these goals? Write also about your fears and resistance in seeking these changes. Fears hold a lot of wisdom, and we can only learn their lessons and move beyond resistance by looking our fears in the eye.

ART AS
MEDITATION

*T*hese are the art projects listed at the end of each chapter. They are designed to bring you into your right brain and to attune you with spirit and nature through art.

- Make an altar, a place to sit outside and be with yourself, write, and listen. This can be as simple as a special chair on your balcony, or a miniature temple carved out of your garden. Let yourself play by listening to the surrounding land and helping it to express its own sacred nature. Include your favorite colors, wind chimes, and anything that helps you feel joy and expansion.

- Another way to witness the body and how we use it to carry our experiences is through art. On a large piece of paper, have a friend trace your body, or draw a rough outline of your body from memory. Ground and center. Fill in the body outline with colors or pictures from magazines that represent how each part of your body feels, or how you feel about that body part. Spend some time on this project, maybe going back to it a couple of times. You may wish to share your Body Map with a trusted friend when you are finished. Discuss or write about what you discover about your body and your relationship with it.

- Make a collage or drawing that you can use in meditation to help align your energies with plant spirits. Tear out favorite pictures of trees, flowers, and other plants from magazines and glue them to a piece of cardstock or construction paper in a mandala or other pleasing arrangement. Or draw your own images, perhaps from your time communicating with plants. Place your art in a spot you see daily, or where you meditate, do ritual, or write in your journal.

- Gather stones, pinecones, shells, or other objects near your home that represent the land around you and your connection with it (ask permission from the land to remove the objects). Collect a few personal items—a strand of your hair, an old earring, or a little totem animal from a bead shop or toy store. Glue these items into a shadow box, or put them in a jar or small box. Decorate the frame, jar, or box with images or colors that say *home* to you. Set your piece on your altar, mantel, or dresser where you can see it. Let it be a totem of home, a symbol of your current connection with this place.

- Craft an item to bless and cleanse, such as a wind chime or Brigit's Cross. A simple chime can be made out of craft glass, shells, little pieces of bamboo, or even old spoons. To make a Brigit's Cross, gather at least nine twelve-inch-long strands of wheat or grass. Historically these were pulled rather than cut. Soak in water to soften, and gather four rubber bands or string to secure the ends. Remove your straw from its bath. Hold two straws vertical, and wrap one around the other at the center to the right, making a sideways *T*-shape. Hold the center tightly and rotate the whole thing ninety degrees counterclockwise. Add another straw, and wrap it around the vertical straw, as in the first step. Repeat the turning and wrapping until you have used all your straw pieces, then secure the ends.

- Pledge your garden to compassionate relationship with the land. Make or decorate an object that symbolizes this dedication, such as a statue, bird bath, bird or bat house, mosaic flower pot, or garden stepping stone. You can purchase kits for simple garden art from hobby shops and good toy stores. Every time you see your garden art, you will be reminded of your work as a garden activist, working to heal the land.

- Make a collage or drawing of your herbal ally. Press a fresh herb between two pieces of waxed paper and leave it in a book for a few weeks until dried.

Glue the pressed herb onto thick cardstock or homemade paper. Frame the herb with descriptive words or phrases that came to you in meditation or that you have learned from books or classes on herbs. Decorate your paper altar with images you draw or cut out from magazines to illustrate the qualities of this plant. Hang your visual homage wherever you work with herbs.

- If you regularly use a substance like cigarettes, wine, or marijuana, create a sacred space to store them. Find a tin or an empty cigar box and decorate it with images of Spirit, the planet, and other things sacred to you. If you have a wine rack or alcohol cabinet, write a prayer about your intent in aligning with your higher power. Write it on decorative paper and place it where you store alcohol. This is not to cover up any unhealthy habits with a pretext of spiritual expansiveness, but to remind you of the possibilities of sacred alignment when working with these substances.

- Using cardboard, paint, sequins, feathers, fabric, markers, and anything else you like, make a Power Animal mask. Using illustrations from books, make a mask that represents the animal that appeared to you in this chapter's meditation. Hang it over your altar or in a place of honor in your house. You may even want to wear it, taking on the qualities of that being. How does it feel to become your power animal? Be sure to return to human form when you are done.

- Make a prayer necklace. Get light-colored, air-hardening clay or another medium of your choice from a local hobby shop. State aloud your intentions for you life and the earth; as you make your beads, hold these intentions in your heart. Roll the clay into little balls, about ¼- to ½-inch in diameter. Poke a toothpick or needle through the middle, wiggling it a little to make the hole large enough to accommodate a string. Let your beads dry for a few days, then paint them with colors that remind you of your path. String them on fishing line or thin leather cord. When you pray or meditate, hold the string of beads in your hands. You can finger a bead at a time like a rosary, wear it on your wrist like a Buddhist mala, or simply hold it to align you with your life work.

SOURCES

Amber K. *Candlemas: Feast of Flames*. St. Paul: Llewellyn, 2003.

Andrews, Lynn. *The Mask of Power: Discovering Your Sacred Self.* San Francisco: Harper SanFrancisco, 1992.

Andrews, Ted. *Animal-Speak: The Spiritual & Magical Powers of Creatures Great & Small.* St. Paul: Llewellyn, 1996.

Buhner, Stephen Harrod. *The Secret Teachings of Plants: The Intelligence of the Heart in the Direct Perception of Nature.* Rochester, VT: Bear & Company, 2004.

Carr-Gomm, Philip and Stephanie. *The Druid Animal Oracle: Working with the Sacred Animals of the Druid Tradition.* New York: Simon and Schuster, 1994.

Ching, Kaleo and Elise Dirlam. *Faces of Your Soul: Rituals in Art, Maskmaking, and Guided Imagery with Ancestors, Spirit Guides, and Totem Animals.* Berkley, CA: North Atlantic Books, 2006.

Chodron, Pema. *The Wisdom of No Escape and the Path of Loving-Kindness.* Boston: Shambhala, 1991.

Conklin, Allis E. "It's a Time for Healing in Dead Zone—Bellingham Works to Get Past the Pipeline Tragedy." *Seattle Post-Intelligencer* (July 3, 1999).

Cunningham, Scott. *Magical Herbalism.* St Paul: Llewellyn, 2002.

Curott, Phyllis. *Witch Crafting: A Spiritual Guide to Making Magic.* New York: Broadway Books, 2001.

Cruden, Loren. *Medicine Grove: A Shamanic Herbal.* Rochester, VT: Destiny Books, 1997.

Danaan, Clea. *Sacred Land: Intuitive Gardening for Personal, Political & Environmental Change.* Woodbury, MN: Llewellyn, 2007.

Davy, Emma. "In Sync," *Current Science* Vol. 87, Issue 7 (11/23/2001).

Fox, Matthew. *A Spirituality Named Compassion and the Healing of the Global Village, Humpty Dumpty and Us.* San Francisco: Harper & Row, 1979.

Gladstar, Rosemary. *Rosemary Gladstar's Family Herbal.* North Adams, MA: Storey Books, 2001.

Haas, Michael J. "One Foot in Each World: Fantasy Writing and Shamanic Journeys," *Shaman's Drum* Number 74 (2007).

Hoffman, David. *The New Holistic Herbal.* New York: Barnes and Noble, 1995.

Ingerman, Sandra. *Medicine for the Earth.* New York: Three Rivers Press, 2001.

Jackson, Wes. *Altars of Unhewn Stone: Science and the Earth.* San Francisco: North Point Press, 1987.

Kingsolver, Barbara. *Animal, Vegetable, Miracle.* New York: Harper Collins, 2007.

Koda, Katalin. *The Sacred Path of Reiki: Healing as a Spiritual Discipline.* Woodbury, MN: Llewellyn, 2008.

L'Engle, Madeleine. *A Circle of Quiet.* Minneapolis: Seabury Press, 1979.

Marion, Jim. *Putting On the Mind of Christ: The Inner Work of Christian Spirituality*. Charlottesville, VA: Hampton Roads, 2000.

Markova, Dawna. *The Art of the Possible: A Compassionate Approach to Understanding the Way People Think, Learn and Communicate*. Berkeley, CA: Conari Press, 1991.

————. *How Your Child Is Smart: A Life-Changing Approach to Learning*. Berkeley, CA: Conari Press, 1992.

McTaggart, Lynne. *The Field: The Quest for the Secret Force of the Universe*. New York, Harper Collins, 2002.

Miller, Julie Ann. "Botanical Divinities." *Science News* Vol. 118 Issue 5 (8/2/1980).

Nelson, Robert T., Jim Brunner, and Steve Miletich. "Lighter Ignited Fire; Bigger Disaster Averted," *The Seattle Times* (June 17, 1999).

Parker, Julia and Derek. *Parker's Astrology: The Definitive Guide to Using Astrology in Every Aspect of Your Life*. New York: DK Publishing, 1994.

Pert, Candace. *Molecules of Emotion: The Science Behind Mind-Body Medicine*. New York: Touchstone, 1999.

Sams, Jamie and David Carson. *Medicine Cards: The Discovery of Power Through the Ways of Animals*. Santa Fe: Bear & Company, 1988.

Schwenk, Theodore. *Sensitive Chaos: The Creation of Flowing Forms in Water and Air*. London: Rudolf Steiner Press, 1990.

Sivin, Carole. *Maskmaking*. New York: Sterling Publishing, 1986.

Starhawk. *The Earth Path: Grounding Your Spirit in the Rhythms of Nature*. San Francisco: Harper SanFrancisco, 2004.

Tolle, Eckhart. *The Power of Now: A Guide to Spiritual Enlightenment.* Novato, CA: New World Library, 1999.

Tompkins, Peter. *The Secret Live of Nature: Living in Harmony with the Hidden World of Nature Spirits from Fairies to Quarks.* New York: Harper SanFrancisco, 1997.

———. *The Secret Life of Plants.* New York: Harper & Row, 1973.

Weed, Susun. *Healing Wise.* Woodstock, NY: Ash Tree Publishing, 1989.

Welwood, John. *Love and Awakening: Discovering the Sacred Path of Intimate Relationship.* New York: Harper Collins, 1997.

Wilber, Ken. *Integral Spirituality: A Startling New Role for Religion in the Modern and Postmodern World.* Boston: Shambhala, 2006.

———. *Sex, Ecology, Spirituality: The Spirit of Evolution.* Boston: Shambhala, 1995.

Wright, Machaelle Small. *Co-Creative Science: A Revolution in Science Providing Real Solutions for Today's Health and Environment.* Warrenton, VA: Perelandra, 1997.

ELECTRONIC SOURCES

Amnesty International. "Democratic Republic of Congo: Government should investigate human rights violations in the Mbuji Mayi diamond fields." Press Release. http://web.amnesty.org/library/Index/ENGAFR620212002?open&of=ENG-398

Ban Cyanide! "Gold Campaign." Rainforest Information Centre. http://www.rainforestinfo.org.au/gold/cyanide.htm

Purdue University Center for New Crops & Plants Products. "Cannabis Sativa L." From James A. Duke, *Handbook of Energy*

Crops, 1983 (unpublished manuscript), http://www.hort. purdue.edu/newcrop/duke_energy/Cannabis_sativa.html

Sayahda. "Cycle of Power, Animal Totems." http://www .sayahda.com/cycle.htm

The Vinegar Institute. "Uses and Tips." http://www .versatilevinegar.org/usesandtips.html

World Research Foundation. "The Electrical Patterns of Life (The Work of Dr. Harold Saxton Burr)." http://www.wrf .org/men-women-medicine/dr-harold-s-burr.php

Wright, Machaelle Small. "A Message from Machaelle." E-mail newsletter. April 23, 2007.

Notes

NOTES

NOTES

NOTES

NOTES

NOTES

NOTES

NOTES

To Write to the Author

If you wish to contact the author or would like more information about this book, please write to the author in care of Llewellyn Worldwide and we will forward your request. Both the author and publisher appreciate hearing from you and learning of your enjoyment of this book and how it has helped you. Llewellyn Worldwide cannot guarantee that every letter written to the author can be answered, but all will be forwarded. Please write to:

Clea Danaan
c/o Llewellyn Worldwide
2143 Wooddale Drive, Dept. 978-0-7387-1465-3
Woodbury, MN 55125-2989, U.S.A.
Please enclose a self-addressed stamped envelope for reply,
or $1.00 to cover costs. If outside U.S.A., enclose
international postal reply coupon.

Many of Llewellyn's authors have websites with additional information and resources. For more information, please visit our website at:

www.llewellyn.com

Free Catalog!

Get the latest information on our body, mind, and spirit products! To receive a **free** copy of Llewellyn's consumer catalog, *New Worlds of Mind & Spirit,* simply call 1-877-NEW-WRLD or visit our website at www.llewellyn.com and click on *New Worlds.*

LLEWELLYN ORDERING INFORMATION

Order Online:
Visit our website at www.llewellyn.com, select your books, and order them on our secure server.

Order by Phone:
- Call toll-free within the U.S. at 1-877-NEW-WRLD (1-877-639-9753). Call toll-free within Canada at 1-866-NEW-WRLD (1-866-639-9753)
- We accept VISA, MasterCard, and American Express

Order by Mail:
Send the full price of your order (MN residents add 6.5% sales tax) in U.S. funds, plus postage & handling to:

> **Llewellyn Worldwide**
> **2143 Wooddale Drive, Dept. 978-0-7387-1465-3**
> **Woodbury, MN 55125-2989**

Postage & Handling:

Standard (U.S., Mexico, & Canada). If your order is:
> $24.99 and under, add $3.00
> $25.00 and over, FREE STANDARD SHIPPING

AK, HI, PR: $15.00 for one book plus $1.00 for each additional book.

International Orders (airmail only):
> $16.00 for one book plus $3.00 for each additional book

Orders are processed within 2 business days.
Please allow for normal shipping time. Postage and handling rates subject to change.

Sacred Land
Intuitive Gardening for Personal, Political and Environmental Change

CLEA DANAAN

Clea Danaan breaks new ground with *Sacred Land*—a fresh approach to sacred gardening that goes beyond the backyard.

Danaan shows how the garden can germinate environmental awareness and political change while feeding the spirit. You'll learn how to create compost, save seeds, connect with garden goddesses, perform rituals and magic, and incorporate planetary energy in the garden. Each of the four sections—spanning earth, air, fire, and water—suggest ways of spreading this message of ecology and sustainability to the community. There are also inspiring stories of activists, farmers, artists, healers and other women who are making a difference in the world.

978-0-7387-1146-1, 336 pp., 5 ³⁄₁₆ x 8 $15.95

Craft of the Wild Witch
Green Spirituality & Natural Enchantment

POPPY PALIN

Wild witchcraft is a magical, free-spirited philosophy that embraces nature. A wildwitch finds magic in the mundane and inspiration in everyday life. Poppy Palin offers us a poetic guidebook to the green-spirited path—where thoughts and deeds become acts of devotion or enchantment. She teaches us how to read nature's language and develop a living relationship with the land. From the perspective of a wildwitch, she reviews enchantment, spellweaving, the fey, companion spirits, intuition development, protection procedures, and much more.

978-0-7387-0577-4, 336 pp., 7½ x 9⅛ $18.95

HedgeWitch
Spells, Crafts & Rituals for Natural Magick

SILVER RAVENWOLF

Get a fast and fun jump-start on the HedgeWitch path with a little help from the immensely popular Silver RavenWolf. Arranged in an easy-to-follow format, this gifty guidebook has everything a new Witch needs to practice the free-spirited, informal garden and cottage-based witchery of Hedge Craft.

At the core of the book is a fourteen-lesson, hands-on guide that readers complete at their own pace, interacting with different aspects of nature in simple yet powerful ways, e.g., performing the Night of the Starry Sky ritual. The lessons, which can be done alone or with a group, culminate in an inspiring dedication ceremony.

A handy reference section offers tips, formulas, recipes, and helpful hints on topics such as soap making, tea leaf reading, butterfly garden magick, and organically growing your own herbs.

978-0-7387-1423-3, 336 pp., 7½ x 9⅛ $18.95

Flower and Tree Magic
Discover the Natural Enchantment Around You

RICHARD WEBSTER

Did you know that flowers have a unique language of their own? Or that the way you draw a tree reflects your life outlook and personality?

Flowers and trees have long been celebrated as sacred and powerful. By learning to read the special messages they hold, plants can help us navigate our life path and reconnect with nature. In this comprehensive guide, bestselling author Richard Webster uncovers the hidden properties of every major type of tree, herb, and flower that we encounter in our daily lives. From protection and healing to divination and worship, this book shows you how to apply ancient spiritual practices from many cultures to modern life—attract your ideal mate with valerian and sage, ward off psychic attacks with a sprinkling of rose oil, restore positive energy with nature meditations, and more.

Nature lovers, myth historians, and trivia lovers alike will embrace this all-encompassing guide to the vast history and extensive magic of flowers and trees.

978-0-7387-1349-6, 240 pp., 6 x 9 $15.95

Ecoshamanism
Sacred Practices of Unity, Power and Earth Healing

JAMES ENDREDY

In a society riddled with rampant consumerism and unsustainable technology, it's easy for everyone, including shamans, to lose touch with the natural world. James Endredy, who has learned from tribal shamans around the globe, presents a new philosophy of shamanic practice called ecological shamanism, or ecoshamanism. Designed to deliver well-being and spiritual harmony, ecoshamanism is the culmination of the visionary practices, rituals, and ceremonies that honor and support nature.

Exploring the holistic perspective of shamanism, Endredy encourages readers to establish a rewarding connection with sacred, life-giving forces using shamanic tools and practices. The author describes more than fifty authentic ecoshamanistic practices—including ceremonies, rituals, chanting, hunting, pilgrimage, and making instruments—that reinforce one's relationship with the natural world.

978-0-7387-0742-6, 360 pp., 7½ x 9⅛ $19.95